CONFEDERATE SEADOG

CONFEDERATE SEADOG

John Taylor Wood in War and Exile

by John Bell

McFarland & Company, Inc., Publishers
Jefferson, North Carolina, and London

Frontispiece: John Taylor Wood, c. 1895 (*Nova Scotia Archives and Records Management, N-1168*).

Library of Congress Cataloguing-in-Publication Data

Bell, John, 1952–
    Confederate seadog : John Taylor Wood in war and exile / by John Bell.
        p.   cm.
    Includes bibliographical references and index.

    ISBN 0-7864-1352-2 (softcover : 50# alkaline paper)

    1. Confederate States of America. Navy — Biography.
2. Confederate States of America. Army.   3. Cavalry — Biography.   4. Ship captains — Confederate States of America — Biography.   5. United States — History — Civil War, 1861–1865 — Naval operations.

E467.1.W86B45   2002
973.7'57'092 — dc21   2002009592

British Library cataloguing data are available

Cover photographs: John Taylor Wood and his ship the CSS *Tallahassee*

Manufactured in the United States of America

McFarland & Company, Inc., Publishers
    Box 611, Jefferson, North Carolina 28640
    www.mcfarlandpub.com

To Arnold Vincent (Ken) Bell and Peter Gerald Rogers,
who heeded the call and served their country.

Acknowledgments

My work on *Confederate Seadog: John Taylor Wood in War and Exile* could not have been completed without the generous assistance of numerous people in the United States and Canada.

First of all, I would like to express my gratitude to three managers at the National Archives of Canada: Peter DeLottinville (chief of the Political Archives Section), Eldon Frost (former director of the Manuscript Division), and Omer Boudreau (director general of the Canadian Archives Branch), all of whom kindly supported my research on this project.

I would also like to thank the staff of the following institutions: the University of North Carolina Manuscripts Department (especially Steven Niven, Laura Clark Brown and Donna Baker), the Virginia State Library, the Museum of the Confederacy, Nova Scotia Archives and Records Management (particularly Philip Hartling and Garry Shutlak), the National Library of Canada (notably Michel Brisebois and Jamie Martin), the National Archives of Canada (in particular my colleagues Pat Kennedy, Myron Momryk, Brian Murphy, and Glenn Wright), Dalhousie University Libraries System (principally Charles Armour and Hansel Cook of the University Archives, and Diane Landry of Special Collections), and the Nova Scotia Museum (especially Valerie Lenethen and Scott Robson).

As well, I would like to express my thanks to Natasha Bell, Laura Bradley (Yarmouth County Museum and Archives), Brian Gomes, Mary E. Herbert (Maryland Historical Society), Lewis Jackson, Leon C. Miller (Tulane University Manuscripts Division), Nancy O'Brien, Jean Rogers, the late Peter G. Rogers, Su Rogers, Michael Rowe, Allan Ruffman, Ted Savas, Carolyn Scott, the late Arthur Thurston, and John Townsend.

Contents

War that terrible calamity is upon us & worst of all among ourselves.
—John Taylor Wood, 13 April 1861

Preface

The American Civil War is generally regarded as the first modern war. A long and bloody conflict that involved more than three million combatants on land, sea, and brown water, it claimed more than 600,000 lives and ushered in a terrible new era of industrial warfare. While not, strictly speaking, a world war, it did have a significant international dimension and at times spilled beyond the borders of the United States. Not surprisingly, given its duration and character, this fratricidal war saw many memorable individuals—from common foot soldiers through to the highest-ranking officers—fight for either the creation of a new Confederate nation or the preservation of the old Union. On the naval side of the conflict, undoubtedly one of the most remarkable participants of all was John Taylor Wood, among the few people to hold dual rank in the Confederate military, serving as a captain in the Confederate States Navy (CSN) and as a cavalry colonel.

A grandson of American President Zachary Taylor and a nephew of the president of the Confederate States of America, Jefferson Davis, Wood was a former United States Navy (USN) officer who emerged as one of the Confederacy's most daring commandos. He also served on the ironclad CSS *Virginia* and later commanded CSS *Tallahassee*, one of the South's most successful commerce raiders. Moreover, as an aide-de-camp to President Davis, Wood participated in various combined operations and provided valuable liaison between the president and Confederate military leaders. In his capacity as a presidential aide, Wood was with Davis when the latter was captured at the end of the war, but managed to escape, making his way to Cuba and then Halifax, Nova Scotia in British North America (now Canada) where he lived out his life in self-imposed exile.

Although John Taylor Wood's wartime activities won him praise from the likes of Jefferson Davis, Robert E. Lee, Mary Boykin Chesnut, and

David Dixon Porter, by the time of his death in 1904 Wood was largely forgotten in his native country — at least outside of Confederate veterans' circles. His passing did prompt the *Times Dispatch* of Richmond to run a small, respectful notice on the bottom of its front page, and perhaps a few other American papers followed suit, but generally speaking, Wood's death, nearly forty years after the war's end, was not a particularly newsworthy event in America.

In his adopted home, on the other hand, Wood's passing was announced in major headlines and detailed in lengthy lead stories. This substantial coverage in the Halifax press reflected the curious fact that over time the unreconstructed Confederate naval hero had been transformed into a Haligonian and Nova Scotian icon. This elevation of Wood to the pantheon of Bluenose heroes continued for many decades after his death, as his connection with the province of Nova Scotia — especially the escape of the CSS *Tallahassee* through Halifax harbor's Eastern Passage — was celebrated in numerous local publications, including school readers. In 1955 his exploits were even commemorated by the opening of the Tallahassee School at Eastern Passage, outside Dartmouth, across the harbor from Halifax. Contributing to Wood's reputation in Nova Scotia and Canada were the achievements of his descendants within the North-West Mounted Police (later Royal Canadian Mounted Police), most notably his son Zachary Taylor Wood, who became the force's assistant commissioner, and his grandson Stuart Taylor Wood, who later served as commissioner.

In the United States, Wood remained a surprisingly marginal figure until the late 1930s, when he was the subject of a thesis, in 1935, by W.D. Harville at the Southern Methodist University in Dallas and of an entry by Confederate naval historian William M. Robinson, Jr., in the *Dictionary of American Biography* (1936). As well, he figured prominently in A.J. Hanna's account of the post-war fate of the members of the Confederate cabinet, *Flight into Oblivion* (1938). Nonetheless, this flurry of attention was not sustained, and it was not until the late 1970s that Wood was finally reclaimed as an important figure in American Civil War history. To a large degree, this rediscovery was due to the efforts of the historian Royce Gordon Shingleton, who first contributed articles on Wood to the *Civil War Times Illustrated* (1976) and *The United Daughters of the Confederacy Magazine* (1978), before publishing the first major biography of the Confederate naval hero, *John Taylor Wood: Sea Ghost of the Confederacy* (1979). Shingleton's book is a first-rate, groundbreaking piece of scholarship; however, it does have some drawbacks, providing scant information on Wood's early life and neglecting certain key aspects of Wood's career in Halifax. As Shingleton himself readily admitted, his book should be viewed primarily as an account of Wood's military career, not as a full-fledged biography.

Shingleton's study was soon followed by a second biography of Wood, Arthur Thurston's *Tallahassee Skipper* (1981), a Nova Scotian publication that is largely unknown in the United States. Thurston's book is a far more ambitious work than Shingleton's biography and has the virtue of drawing on numerous Canadian sources that were not utilized by Shingleton. Unfortunately, the book is deeply flawed and far from reliable. Although he was in some respects a dogged researcher, Thurston, who died a few years ago, was an extremely eccentric individual, and his book suffers from an exceedingly speculative and undisciplined approach to historiography, as well as a meandering writing style. Unlike Shingleton, Thurston's use of sources is frequently undocumented and sometimes questionable. His book contains some useful information, but must be approached with caution.

Since the appearance of Shingleton and Thurston's biographies, Wood has been the subject of numerous articles (based mostly on secondary sources) in popular Civil War periodicals such as *Civil War Times Illustrated* and *America's Civil War*. As well, he has figured prominently in recent writing about the CSN commerce raiders and in Raimondo Luraghi's authoritative *A History of the Confederate Navy* (1996). Clearly, Wood is now a figure of considerable renown, especially in the burgeoning field of Civil War naval history.

Although a substantial body of writing has been devoted to Wood during the past two decades or so, some significant oversights are evident in this literature. First of all, the best of the war-related memoirs that Wood contributed to *The Century Illustrated Monthly Magazine* and other periodicals have not been collected. Secondly, apart from Arthur Thurston's idiosyncratic work, no concerted effort has been made to employ the Canadian (particularly Nova Scotian) primary and secondary sources that would permit a fuller description of Wood's post-war life. Finally, there remains a number of U.S. sources (the most significant being a previously undiscovered autobiographical manuscript by Wood) that have not hitherto been drawn upon to provide a more complete picture of Wood's life before the war, as well as a more accurate account of his wartime service.

The work at hand, *Confederate Seadog: John Taylor Wood in War and Exile*, attempts to redress these shortcomings in the published record relating to Wood. The book is divided into two main sections. The first part, "Under Three Flags: The Life and Legacy of John Taylor Wood," consists of a lengthy biographical essay on Wood that makes use of several important primary sources that were either unavailable to, or overlooked by, previous researchers. "Under Three Flags" offers important new details regarding Wood's childhood and youth, such as his harrowing experiences in Florida during the Seminole Wars. As well, it sheds new light on his USN service during and immediately after the Mexican War (most notably, perhaps, his experiences in California during the gold rush) and provides some additional details regarding his Civil War career. The essay also contains new information regarding Wood's leading role among the members of the little-known Confederate naval colony that took shape in Halifax, Nova Scotia following the war, including his efforts in 1866 to arrange for himself and other Confederate expatriates to fight for Britain against the Fenian forces (mostly Union veterans) then threatening British North America. Finally, the essay offers the first full account of Wood's writings relating to the war and his other literary activities, and reveals many other overlooked facts about his later life, including, for instance, his friendship with William Hall, the first black to win the Victoria Cross.

The second part, "The Civil War Memoirs of a Confederate Exile," collects, for the first time, Wood's best Civil War memoirs, together with the impressive illustrations that accompanied the articles when they originally appeared in *Century* magazine as part of that periodical's famous series of "war papers." Published between 1885 and 1898, these narratives cover his service on the CSS *Virginia* ("The First Fight of Iron-Clads"), the cruise of the CSS *Tallahassee* ("The *Tallahassee's* Dash into New York Waters"), and his remarkable escape from the South as the Confederacy collapsed ("Escape of the Confederate Secretary of War"). These texts, which are preceded by introductory headnotes, afford readers a welcome opportunity to encounter Wood's own voice as he recounts some of his most dramatic experiences of the Civil War.

In addition to these two main sections, the book includes four appendices and an annotated bibliography. The appendices consist of J. Thomas Scharf's account of Wood's capture of the USS *Underwriter* (regrettably, Wood himself did not leave reminiscences touching on his experiences as a commando leader), a listing of the CSS *Tallahassee's* captures, the text of Confederate naval poet E. King's long-forgotten song dedicated to the crew of the CSS *Tallahassee*, and an annotated listing of Wood's own published and unpublished writings. The book's annotated bibliography not only identifies works that were consulted in the preparation of *Confederate Seadog* but also surveys the available secondary literature relating to Wood.

Taken together, the various sections of this intentionally hybrid volume are meant to complement the work that has already been published on Wood — especially Shingleton's excellent biography. Hopefully, *Confederate Seadog* will contribute to a more complete picture of the life of a man

who was not only one of the Confederacy's most-accomplished naval commanders, but also one of Nova Scotia's most-admired Victorian heroes.
By pointing to numerous primary and secondary sources that are largely
unknown to American researchers, it might also encourage future research
on Wood and his singular cross-border career and legacy. John Taylor
Wood's life, shaped to a large degree by duty, courage, faith, and ultimately
exile, certainly merits further attention and serves as a salient reminder
that the Civil War had a significant and lasting impact on America's neigh-
bor to the North.

John Bell

PART ONE

Under Three Flags:
The Life and Legacy of
John Taylor Wood

Chapter 1

A Forgotten Confederate Colony

The end of the American Civil War in 1865 resulted in a significant exodus of Confederate military and political leaders and personnel from the Southern states. Many of the refugees fled possible prosecution for their wartime activities; others were loath to submit to Yankee rule. Joining them in exile were many of the consuls and other agents who had represented the Confederacy abroad.

One of the principal destinations for the fleeing Confederates was the British North American province of Canada (then comprising Canada East and West; now the Canadian provinces of Quebec and Ontario), where there had been considerable sympathy for the South during its struggle with the Northern states.[1] Among the many Confederates who resided for at least a time in Canada were such notables as President Jefferson Davis; Secretary of War John C. Breckinridge; diplomatic commissioner James M. Mason; Generals George Pickett and Jubal Early; Brigadier Generals Danville Leadbetter, William Preston, and John McCausland; acting Brigadier General Edwin Gray Lee; Senator William E. Simms; congressmen Henry S. Foote, Samuel Augustine Miller, William S. Oldham, and Charles Wells Russell; home-front leader Louisa Cheves McCord; and Charles J. Helm, the former Confederate consul in Havana.[2] Many of these exiles were welcomed and assisted by the Toronto lawyer George T. Denison later a renowned military historian and theorist, whose profound dislike of the Yankees made him a natural ally of the Confederates both during and after the Civil War.[3]

Although most of the Confederate refugees in British North America gravitated to the province of Canada, particularly the cities of Montreal and Toronto, a little-known colony of Confederates was established on the east coast of British North America in the province of Nova Scotia. While the Confederate refugees in Nova Scotia included some army personnel — most notably, the Kentucky cavalry colonel Bennett Hornsby and the controversial surgeon in charge of the hospitals at Andersonville Prison, Dr. R. Randolph Stevenson — the majority were former officers of the Confederate Navy, who were naturally drawn to a province with a strong maritime and naval tradition.[4] Most of the east-coast Confederates settled in Nova Scotia's capital and largest city, the port of Halifax, which was home to Britain's North Atlantic Squadron. A few lived across Halifax harbor in the town of Dartmouth.

Many of those involved in the Confederacy's international operations were, of course, already familiar with Halifax. During the Civil War, the city had served as an important fuelling station and repair depot for blockade runners. Furthermore, countless Confederates had passed through the port on their way to and from Europe or Canada. Among the many Southern visitors to Halifax during the war years were the spy Rose O'Neal Greenhow; the noted Confederate States Navy (CSN) commodore, Matthew Fontaine Maury; the founder of the Confederate Secret Service Corps, Captain Thomas E. Courtenay; the Copperhead leader Clement L. Vallandigham; and the Confederate commissioners to Canada, Clement C. Clay, Jacob Thompson, and James P. Holcombe.[5]

Halifax had also figured in three CSN operations that had placed strains on Anglo-American relations. In October 1863, the city served as the launching point for the ill-fated attempt to free the Southerners imprisoned on Johnson's Island in Lake Eerie. Later that same year, Halifax was caught up in the so-called Chesapeake Affair, after Confederate sympathizers, including several Nova Scotians, seized the U.S. coastal steamer *Chesapeake* and sailed the vessel into British waters, where she was illegally recaptured by the USS *Ella and Annie*. In August 1864, Halifax was at the center of yet another flurry of British and American diplomatic activity when the cruiser CSS *Tallahassee* put into the port for coal and repairs after successfully preying on Union shipping on the east coast of the United States for twelve days.[6]

The post-war colony of Southerners in Halifax and Dartmouth counted among its members some of the Confederacy's leading naval officers, including Commodore Josiah Tattnall; Colonel (Cavalry) and Captain (Navy) John Taylor Wood (commander of the *Tallahassee*); Captain John Wilkinson (leader of the Johnson Island expedition); Commander George T. Sinclair; Lieutenants Frank Lyell Hoge, Richard Fielder Armstrong, and William H. Sinclair; Midshipmen Gilbert A. Wilkins and George L. Sinclair; and Chief Engineer Charles Schroeder. These navy veterans were joined by several other Confederates, including Marine Corps Captain John R.F. Tattnall, the son of Josiah Tattnall; George P. Black, one of the Confederacy's agents in Bermuda; Jacob Thompson, a former Confederate commissioner to Canada and, for a time, a suspected conspirator in the Lincoln assassination; and Dr. William Bruce Almon, a Nova Scotian who had served with the Confederate Army and whose father, Dr. William J. Almon, was one of British North America's most rabid supporters of the Confederacy.[7]

Over time, most of the Confederate refugees in Nova Scotia and the other British North American provinces drifted back to the Southern states, prompted by homesickness and Federal offers of pardons. However, several Nova Scotian Confederates did choose to stay in their adopted home, determined to remain in exile from an America dominated by the Yankee victors of the Civil

The firm Wilkinson, Wood and Company brought together three of Halifax's Confederate exiles (*McAlpine's Nova Scotia Directory for 1869-69*).

War. By far the most prominent of these unreconstructed rebels was John Taylor Wood, one of the few people to hold rank in both the Confederate States Navy and the Army. Even though he never formally became a British subject, Wood heartily embraced his new homeland, becoming a Bluenose patriot and emerging as one of the leading citizens of Nova Scotia during the Victorian era.

Chapter 2

Early Life, 1830–1847

Fittingly for a man who would become one of the Confederacy's most daring warriors, John Taylor Wood grew up against the backdrop of war. Born at Fort Snelling in the Northwest Territory (now St. Paul, Minnesota) on 13 August 1830, Wood was the first child of Robert Crooke Wood, an assistant surgeon in the U.S. Army, and Anne Mckall Taylor, the daughter of "Old Rough and Ready," General Zachary Taylor, who was then commander of the U.S. forces stationed at the remote military post. According to Wood, his first memory was of "the weird crooning against the Sioux" by the Winnebago woman who served as his nurse.[8] It is generally assumed that Wood was the first white child born in Minnesota.

From about 1832 to 1837, Wood's family lived at Fort Crawford (now Prairie du Chien, Wisconsin). During these years his grandfather and father were involved in the efforts to assert American authority over the various Indian nations living in the vast northwestern frontier (comprising present-day Ohio, Indiana, Illinois, Michigan, Wisconsin, and portions of Minnesota). The most violent episode during this period was the Black Hawk War, an uprising of the Sac and Fox Indians led by Chief Black Hawk. It was during this conflict that a young officer named Jefferson Davis was stationed at Fort Crawford, where he courted Zachary Taylor's second daughter, Sarah Knox Taylor. When the couple married on 17 June 1835, Davis became Wood's uncle.[9]

In the spring of 1837, the Taylor and Wood families left Fort Crawford. Their ultimate destination was distant Florida, where the Seminole War was raging. However, before assuming his new duties, Zachary Taylor was granted several months' leave. Wood's extended family and their servants and belongings were loaded into a 40-foot, largely open Mackinaw boat for an eighteen-day trip down the Mississippi through hostile Indian country to St. Louis. For six-year-old Wood it was a thrilling adventure. The

"Old Rough and Ready," John Taylor Wood's grandfather, the war hero Zachary Taylor (*1863 engraving from the author's collection*).

party traveled only by day and chose campsites for the night with a view to their defensive potential. The men often hunted for wild game, and young John participated in two exciting chases in small birchbark canoes, pursuing deer that were attempting to swim the river. During one chase, he later recalled, "an old buck made a gallant fight and though wounded, capsized the canoe with his antlers, swamping it and throwing the half-breed out who, coming to the surface, grabbed him by his mane, straddled him, and drawing his knife, cut his throat."[10]

After spending the summer in Kentucky, the family embarked for Florida. In order to negotiate the Ohio River, which was abnormally low, Wood's grandfather bought a flat boat and partially covered the after section. The journey down the Ohio was difficult and laborious. The boat grounded frequently on sand bars, resulting in numerous delays. When the family finally reached Cairo, they were happy to exchange their cramped quarters for the relative luxury of a large river boat, which took them to New Orleans. Next, they booked passage on a small brig loaded with army stores. This proved to be an ordeal. After a twelve-day, wretched voyage in the foul-smelling cargo vessel, they arrived at Tampa Bay, and their final destination: Fort Brooke.[11]

At Forts Snelling and Crawford, the Indian Wars had occupied the background of Wood's life. Fort Brooke was a different matter. Wood's new home was at the center of a brutal war brought on, in his words, by "the land craze of the whites." The fort encompassed about three acres and was surrounded by a stockade, except for the water side, which was open. It was often threatened by attack. In fact, just before Wood's arrival, the Seminoles had ambushed two companies of soldiers nearby, killing more than one hundred men. During the time that the Wood family was there, the women and children were frequently left alone for extended periods, with only a small guard to protect them. In the absence of Wood's father and grandfather, the vulnerable family came to rely on the guidance of a male black servant.[12]

The only well water inside the fort was brackish, which meant that dangerous forays had to be made from the fort to an outside well about half a mile away. On one of these trips, two men were captured and scalped within sight of Fort Brooke. On another occasion, a captured soldier who had survived a massacre and was on the verge of being tortured, managed to escape and return to the fort. He had effected his escape by feverishly working the buckskin thongs that bound him, cutting his shoulders and wrists through to the bone. "His appearance," Wood later wrote, "will never be effaced from my memory."[13]

In 1839, Wood's father was ordered to the Buffalo Barracks at Buffalo,

New York, where he served as Post Surgeon. Compared to Wood's early years, his family's new life was quiet and uneventful. All that changed, however, in 1846, when Robert Wood was called upon to once again join his father-in-law, who was then on the Rio Grande, engaged in the early stages of the Mexican War. Not long after the war started, John turned sixteen. Bored with his life in Buffalo, he was increasingly eager to join his father and grandfather. He would soon have his wish. Young John Taylor Wood was about to become a sailor, embarking on a career that would bring him both notoriety and glory.[14]

Chapter 3

United States Navy, 1847–1861

On 7 April 1847 Wood was appointed a midshipman in the United States Navy from the Newport District of Kentucky, his grandfather's home state. Following a brief preparatory course at the Annapolis Naval School (later Academy), he was ordered to the frigate *Brandywine*, then fitting out at Norfolk as a flagship for the Brazil Station. Upon his arrival at Rio de Janeiro, after a slow, ninety-day voyage, Wood was "right glad" to be transferred with four or five mess-mates to the line-of-battle ship *Ohio*, bound for the Pacific and the Mexican War.[15]

The *Ohio* reached the West coast of Mexico in the latter part of 1847. To Wood's "great joy," his division was selected to join a force of 1000 sailors landed to capture the port of Mazzatan. Although the Americans met with little serious resistance, there were regular skirmishes around the town, particularly at some of the Navy's more remote outposts. It was here that Wood, who was placed in charge of an outpost with a gun crew of twelve men, got his first taste of combat, daily exchanging shots with Mexican forces. "One day," he later recalled, "we coaxed a squadron of cavalry within range by first firing with small charges falling short of their position and then opening on them with full charges."[16]

With the end of the Mexican War in the summer of 1848, Wood returned to the *Ohio*, which engaged in fleet maneuvers before calling on La Paz and San Jose, where the vessel took on board garrison troops and U.S. loyalists for transportation to Monterey. Not long after the *Ohio's* arrival in California, the state was swept up in the chaos of the gold rush. The *Ohio* proceeded to San Francisco Bay, where the Navy, beset by desertions and even mutiny, endeavored to impose some order.[17]

For Wood and the crew of *Ohio*, San Francisco proved to be a far more dangerous place than Mexico. During this period, Wood found himself a member of a party of seven dispatched to the mean streets of San Francisco to arrest a deserter who had been involved in the murder of a midshipman. The sailors were led to a ramshackle, smoke-filled gambling den crowded with more than thirty armed men. Midshipman Wood watched with amazement as the lieutenant in charge of his party boldly stared down the desperados and succeeded in arresting and removing the deserter. "I do not know," Wood later wrote, "of a more striking example of the influence of a personality than in this." John Taylor Wood was learning the skills that would make him an exceptional leader of men.[18]

In the summer of 1849, the difficult situation facing the crew of the *Ohio* deteriorated further. For over a year, the men had been living primarily on salt provisions, with the inevitable result that there was a major outbreak of scurvy. Unable to purchase supplies in San Francisco, the ship left for the Sandwich Islands (Hawaiian Islands) in order to obtain fresh food and permit the crew to recuperate. After calling at Honolulu and Kahaino, the *Ohio* anchored in an isolated bay at Hilo on the Island of Hawaii. Here they found an abundance of fruit and vegetables and a small native community that befriended the exhausted sailors.[19]

While at Hilo, Wood and some of his shipmates climbed the volcanic crater at Kilauea, spending two days observing "the greatest wonder in the world." After two months of welcome rest and relaxation, the *Ohio's* crew were forced to leave their Hawaiian paradise and return to San Francisco. During the voyage back to California, the *Ohio* rescued two Japanese sailors, the only survivors of a disaster that saw their small coastal vessel drift for 140 days across 3,000 miles of ocean. Not long after her arrival at San Francisco, the *Ohio* was relieved by the frigate USS *Savannah*. As a result of desertions and other factors, it was necessary for the *Ohio* to take a draft of fifty sailors from her relief vessel. Among the draftees was a black seaman, William Hall, whom Wood would meet again, years later in Nova Scotia, where the two naval veterans would become friends.[20]

With her homeward-bound pennant flying, the *Ohio* sailed for Boston in November 1849. Four months later, the vessel put into Rio de Janeiro, which was then in the grip of the Yellow Fever. Despite taking precautions, the *Ohio* was unable to avoid the virulent disease. During her return voyage, she lost five officers, several seamen, and two of the vessel's three doctors. Wood was among the last to contract the disease. Fortunately for him, by then the ship's supply of purgatives had been exhausted, and the only remaining doctor was too busy to bleed him.[21]

Yellow Jack was not the only misfortune to befall the *Ohio* on her return voyage. Not far from her destination, the ship grounded on a shoal off

Nantucket. After some anxious hours, she was able to recover and continue on to Boston, where the crew was paid off, and where Wood was granted a three months' leave of absence. He was extremely eager to join his family in Baltimore, where his father was stationed. During Wood's nearly three years at sea, his grandfather had become president of the United States.[22]

In the late spring and early summer of 1850, Wood was a frequent visitor to the White House, where he was given a bedroom on the second floor, immediately over the main entrance, enabling him to "watch the ebb and flow of visitors." In addition to observing his grandfather's daily routine, Wood regularly visited Congress, which was then engaged in a round of fierce debates over the extension of slavery into the territories acquired in the course of the Mexican War. On 4 July, however, partisan wrangling was put aside for a day, and Wood was on hand as his grandfather presided over the laying of the cornerstone for the Washington Monument. By the end of the ceremonies on that intensely hot summer day, Zachary Taylor was obviously not well. A few days later, he was dead. Wood was devastated. "A blow so sudden, so unexpected," he wrote, "overwhelmed the family with grief." However, Wood's time for mourning was limited. His first leave was about to end.[23]

After returning to Annapolis, Wood spent a few months at the Academy before being ordered to the sloop-of-war *Germantown*, which was then at the New York Navy Yard, preparing for a voyage to the coast of Africa. Just as the vessel was about to leave, Spanish-American tensions over Cuba flared, forcing Wood and his messmates to spend a bitterly cold winter in New York awaiting orders. Finally, in the spring of 1851, the vessel departed for Africa, where it joined the American and British naval forces then cooperating in the suppression of the slave trade.[24]

Once on the African coast, Wood was transferred to a small brig, the *Porpoise*. He was decidedly unimpressed with his new vessel: "She was so slow that we could hardly hope for a prize except by a fluke." However, after many unsuccessful chases, the ship did manage to make a capture, overtaking a Spanish slave ship in the Gulf of Guinea. Wood was given command of the captured slaver and ordered to deliver the vessel's human cargo to Monrovia in Liberia. As the *Porpoise* drew away from the Spanish brig, Wood was suddenly struck by the magnitude of his new responsibility: "a young midshipman, ... commanding a prize, with three hundred and fifty prisoners on board, two or three weeks' sail from port, with only a small crew."[25]

The return voyage was not an easy one. On the fifth day out, the ship encountered a severe tropical storm. As the crew struggled throughout the night, Wood passed many anxious hours, "most concerned about the poor creatures under hatches, whose sufferings must have been terrible." Under Wood's guidance, the brig and its passengers survived, reaching Monrovia several days later. For the first time in a fortnight, the young midshipman enjoyed a good night's sleep. However, the morning brought with it new problems. After spending a frustrating day dealing with Monrovia's officialdom and political elite, Wood learned that he could not land his captives in the Liberian capital. Instead, he was forced to take them about a hundred and fifty miles eastward to Grand Bassa. Here he ran into more obstacles, but chose this time to assert himself and land the slaves. From Grand Bassa, Wood returned briefly to Monrovia and then proceeded to Porto Praya, on Cape de Verde Islands, where he reported to the British Commodore. The burden of leadership was now easing for the young midshipman, and it was with great reluctance that he gave up his first command and returned to the *Porpoise*.[26]

Wood returned to the Naval Academy on 1 October 1852 and graduated the following June, placing second in his class. He then served for about two years on the sloop-of-war *Cumberland* in the Mediterranean, before returning again to the Academy, where he was promoted lieutenant as of 16 September 1855. In November 1856, he married Lola Mackubin, the daughter of one of Maryland's most prominent state officials. The couple's first child, Anne Mackall Wood, was born on 18 September 1857.[27]

In June 1858 Wood shipped as a gunnery officer on the steam frigate *Wabash*, the flagship of the Mediterranean Squadron. For the first time in his naval career, he was leaving behind a family. During the eighteen-month cruise, an increasingly homesick Wood wrote Lola more than one hundred sequentially numbered letters.[28] In August 1859, his discouragement deepened with the news that his daughter had died. On 12 August he tenderly assured Lola that little Anne was "among the Angels & will be the first to welcome us to that blessed abode." The following month, he bemoaned his prospects in the Navy: "I see no probability or hardly a possibility of my being anything else than a Lieut. for *twenty* years to come. For that length of time I am called upon to sacrifice health, comfort, family, everything that makes life enjoyable."[29]

When the *Wabash* stood into New York in December 1859, Wood was determined to steer his Navy career in a new direction. Early in the new year he applied for an instructorship at the Academy. To improve his chances, he and his father (now a colonel) lobbied vigorously in Washington. Their efforts were successful. In late February, Wood was appointed an instructor in naval gunnery. Shortly after, he was also given responsibility for seamanship and naval tactics. In the absence of proper texts, he was obliged to compile and translate course material.[30]

Lt. John Taylor Wood, USN, c. 1858 (*The Century Illustrated Monthly Magazine*).

In addition to his teaching duties, Wood was learning to be a gentleman farmer, spending time, whenever possible, at Woodland, a small farm that he had purchased outside Annapolis. While Wood was generally comfortable in his new dual role, he was becoming increasingly uneasy about political developments. He often traveled to Washington and witnessed the rancorous debates in the House of Representatives and the Senate, where his uncle, Jefferson Davis, had emerged as a Democratic leader. In June 1860, another uncle, Richard Taylor, invited Wood to attend the Democratic convention in Baltimore, which saw the party split along sectional lines, yet another sign of a looming tragedy.[31]

On 9 August 1860, Wood was chosen to escort President John Buchanan during the latter's visit to Annapolis. Later that month, Wood embarked on a Western tour, during which he visited three of his previous homes: Fort Snelling, Prairie du Chien, and Buffalo. Following his return, Wood resumed his duties at the Academy. A few months later, on 11 November, his son, Zachary, was born. Wood's joy was tempered by his increasing anxiety over his country's future. Five days earlier, Abraham Lincoln had been elected president, prompting Wood to confide in his diary: "This is as important & eventful a day as has occurred in the annals of our country. I hope & pray it is not the last one of a united country."[32]

Wood's worst fears were soon realized. Starting with South Carolina on 20 December, the seven states of the Lower South passed ordinances of secession. In February 1861 the Confederate States of America was founded at a convention at Montgomery, where Wood's uncle, Jefferson Davis, was elected provisional president. These national divisions were soon reflected in Wood's family: his brother, Robert Crooke Wood, Jr., and his uncle, Richard Taylor, chose to serve the new Confederacy; whereas his parents and his wife's family remained loyal to the Union. Meanwhile, at the Academy, students and staff from the South left for their home states, and within Maryland, a deeply divided border state, sectional strife intensified.[33]

As his world unraveled, Wood struggled to remain neutral. Even though Jefferson Davis had urged him to join the Confederate cause in January, Wood was loath to take up arms in the coming conflict. Events, however, were overtaking him. On 12 April, the bombardment of Fort Sumter began. The following day, Wood confided in his diary that the news "has made me sick at heart." On 15 April, Lincoln called for 75,000 volunteers to put down the Southern rebellion. A few days later, large numbers of federal troops began arriving in Maryland, a move that Wood regarded as a hostile invasion. On 21 April, the day that the Annapolis training ship, USS *Constitution*, was taken to Newport, where the Naval Academy was to be relocated, Wood's blood was "boiling over with indignation," and he resigned his commission. A spiteful Navy Department later backdated his dismissal to 2 April.[34]

During the following months, Wood's life of neutrality quickly became untenable. As a result of his resignation, he and his father soon broke off all contact. Not long after, Wood found himself in a conflict with one of Lola's uncles. As loyalists and secessionists clashed throughout Maryland, travel was becoming dangerous. Fearing for his family's safety, Wood bought a gun. To make matters worse, on several occasions Federal marauders visited the Mackubin family plantation, at Strawberry Hill, where Wood and his family lived for a time following their departure from Annapolis. After the Union defeat at Bull Run, Federal troops also stepped up their arrests of Marylanders suspected of treason.[35]

By the end of August, Wood realized that he would not be able to avoid the vortex of war. After tidying up his affairs at Woodland, he returned to Elk Ridge, where he and his family were then staying. On 3 September, he buried the family silver, later noting in his diary: "I trust it may remain there safe until the times are settled." He then headed south with Lola and their son, Zachary, crossing the Potomac River at night in a small open boat. It proved to be an unexpectedly dangerous voyage. Caught in a sudden storm, Wood was forced to jettison much of their baggage to avoid swamping. After reaching the Virginia shore in Westmoreland County, Wood and his family made their way to the Confederate capital.[36]

Forced by circumstances to choose, Wood finally sided with his Southern heritage and with the cause that had been embraced by two of his uncles, his brother, and many of his Navy colleagues. Serving the Confederacy became the honorable thing to do, especially after the contemptuous treatment he had received at the hands of the United States Navy. Besides, it would surely be a short war, and one that the South, with its superior military traditions, was bound to win.

Chapter 4

Confederate States Navy, 1861–1865

Appointed a lieutenant in the Confederate States Navy as of 4 October, Wood first saw action on the Potomac River, where, during most of the first year of the war, Confederate land batteries effectively blockaded Washington, much to the embarrassment of the Federal government.[37] From September through to the end of 1861, Wood served at the Evansport and Aquia Creek batteries on the Virginia side, below Washington. He later recounted his successes against Union shipping: "While stationed on the river, [I] destroyed several transports and vessels of the enemy, the largest of which was the ship 'Rappahannock' of 1200 tons."[38] During Wood's time on the Potomac, the Union aviator Thaddeus Lowe made several observations of Confederate batteries from a balloon launched from the *G. W. Parke Custis*. This revolutionary use of a ship as an aircraft carrier signaled that the war was rapidly ushering in an era of technological innovation, a development that would have a significant impact on the Confederate States Navy and on John Taylor Wood's career.[39]

In January 1862, Wood was assigned to the CSS *Virginia*, the Confederacy's first ironclad, which was then under construction at the Gosport Navy Yard, utilizing the salvaged hull of the USS *Merrimack*. Wood's first responsibility was to visit various army commands in Virginia in an effort to find experienced seamen or gunners. Once he had selected about three hundred men, Wood took charge of their training. Although he had serious misgivings about the seaworthiness of the *Virginia*, Wood was pleased with the crew he had managed to assemble: "They proved themselves to be as gallant and trusty a body of men as any one would wish to command."[40]

On 8 March the *Virginia*, under the command of Commodore Franklin Buchanan, steamed down the Elizabeth River on her maiden

The CSS Virginia passing the Confederate battery on Craney Island, on her way to attacking the Federal fleet (*The Century Illustrated Monthly Magazine*).

voyage. Wood was in charge of the ironclad's after pivot-gun, a seven-inch Brooke rifle. Upon reaching Hampton Roads, the *Virginia* boldly headed for the Union fleet. She first attacked the sloop of war USS *Cumberland* (on which Wood had once served), ramming and sinking the union warship. The ironclad then turned to confront the frigate USS *Congress*. The *Virginia's* first shots against the frigate were from Wood's pivot-gun. "As we swung," he later recounted, "the *Congress* came in range, nearly stern on, and we got in three raking shells. She had slipped her anchor, loosed her foretop-sail, run up the jib, and tried to escape, but grounded. Turning, we headed for her and took a position within two hundred yards, where every shot told."[41]

The *Congress* finally surrendered, but Union shore positions continued to fire on the *Virginia* and her consort vessels, forcing the Confederates to use hot fire to destroy the union warship. During this latter action, Commodore Buchanan was severely wounded, and command of the *Virginia* passed to Lieutenant Catesby Jones. The *Virginia's* next target was the frigate *Minnesota*, which had grounded not far up the channel from the burning *Congress*. By this time, however, it was almost night, and the tide was low, so it was decided to postpone the attack until the following morning.

At daybreak on 9 March, the Confederates discovered a "strange-looking craft" lying between them and the *Minnesota*. It was the *Monitor*, the first Union ironclad, which had arrived during the night. Later that morning, the two vessels clashed in one of the most significant battles in naval history. During the course of the duel, the *Monitor* directed two point-blank shots abreast of Wood's after pivot. For Wood, it was a close call: "All the crews of the after guns were knocked over by the concussion and bled from the nose or ears. Another shot at the same place would have penetrated."[42] Wood and his crew recovered and were responsible for a well-placed shot that struck the observation slit of the Monitor's pilot house, blinding the Union commander, Lieutenant John L. Worden. By the early afternoon, when the *Monitor* had temporarily withdrawn from the engagement and the tide was falling, it was apparent that the fight was over, and the *Virginia* steamed home to Norfolk.

Although the two vessels had fought to a draw, the *Virginia's* two-day battle with the Union blockading fleet was celebrated as a major victory in the South, and Wood was given the honor of reporting on the encounter to President Davis and members of the Confederate Cabinet. On his train journey to the capital, Wood found himself swarmed by ecstatic Southerners: "The news had preceded me, and at every station I was warmly received, and to listening crowds was forced to repeat the story of the fight."[43]

Wood then returned to Norfolk, where the *Virginia* was placed under the command of Commodore Josiah Tattnall. After undergoing repairs, the ironclad made several unsuccessful attempts in April and May to force another engagement with the *Monitor* and the Union naval forces. On 9 May, Tattnall was shocked to learn that the Confederates had evacuated Norfolk, thereby abandoning his vessel. When it became apparent that the ironclad's excessive draft prevented her ascent of the James River, Tattnall ordered the *Virginia* run ashore near Craney's Island and destroyed. Wood and Catesby Jones were the last to leave the ironclad: "Setting her on fire fore and aft, she was soon in a blaze, and by the light of our burning ship we pulled for the shore, landing at daybreak."[44]

Even without a vessel, the *Virginia's* crew would have one more encounter with the *Monitor*. Rushed by rail to Richmond, which was then being threatened by advancing Union forces under General McClellan, the seamen were put to work preparing defenses on the south bank of the James at Drewery's Bluff, seven miles below the capital. For Wood and his shipmates it was back-breaking, dirty work: "Here, for two days, exposed to constant rain, in bottomless mud and without shelter, on scant provisions, we worked unceasingly, mounting guns and obstructing the river."[45]

On 15 May 1862 two Federal ironclads, the *Galena* and the *Monitor*, and three wooden warships hove in sight. As soon as they were in range, Confederate gunners opened fire. Unable to either pass the obstructions in the river or elevate their guns sufficiently to return effective fire, the Federal vessels soon found themselves in an unequal contest. The Union ships were further harassed by constant fire from a force of sharpshooters commanded by Wood and positioned on the opposite bank of the James. Wood's role in the battle earned the praise of Lieutenant Catesby Jones: "The enemy was excessively annoyed by their fire. His position was well chosen and gallantly maintained in spite of the shell, shrapnel, grape, and canister fired at them."[46] After a battle of four hours, the small Union fleet was forced to retreat. As the federal naval forces retired, Wood, realizing that a former Annapolis colleague was commanding the *Monitor,* called out from the shore: "Tell Captain Jeffers that is not the way to Richmond."[47]

Wood remained stationed at Drewery's Bluff (sometimes referred to as Fort Darling) through the late spring and summer of 1862.[48] Between May and July, the Confederates, first under Joseph E. Johnston, and then under Robert E. Lee and Stonewall Jackson, fought a series of bloody battles with McClellan's Army of the Potomac. Wood was overwhelmed by the resulting carnage: "Our loss has been frightful & grieves me greatly, the best blood of the land has been poured out in torrents; thousands of homes have been made desolate ... No one can describe the horrors & torments of the hospitals in & around Richmond. The air of some of them is sickening [;] it requires a strong head to breathe the air polluted by hundreds of festering wounds."[49] Although the price was high, the outnumbered Confederate forces succeeded in thwarting the Union attempt to take the capital.

Once McClellan's Peninsular Campaign against Richmond ended, service at Drewery's Bluff became too predictable for Wood, who had developed an appetite for action and also become convinced that "promotion as a reward for distinguished services in battle will be the making of our service ... otherwise the Navy never can be kicked into vitality."[50] Stephen Mallory, the Confederate Secretary of the Navy, shared this conviction. On 29 September, Wood was promoted first lieutenant, in recognition of his service on the *Virginia.*[51] A few days later, with Mallory's blessing, he embarked on the first of several daring commando raids that would earn him the nickname "The Horse Marine."[52]

Traveling with whaleboats carried on specially fitted army wagons, Wood and his commando force left Richmond on 1 October and headed north to the Potomac, where they spent several days searching for potential cutting-out victims. On 7 October, they discovered the transport schooner *Frances Elmore* anchored off Pope's Creek on the Maryland side of the river. That night Wood led his men in an attack on the vessel. Armed with swords and pistols, the raiders quickly scrambled over the schooner's side and subdued her hapless captain and crew. Once the *Frances Elmore* was stripped, Wood ordered her burned. He then took his prisoners to Richmond, where they were delivered to Libby Prison.[53]

Emboldened by his first success, Wood quickly organized another expedition, with Lieutenant Sydney Lee as his second in command. This time he headed east from Richmond to Mathews County, Virginia, on the Chesapeake. Here Wood impressed a local pilot and began searching at night for prey, often in very dirty weather. Finally, on the night of 28 October, the commandos sighted the merchant ship *Alleganian* anchored off Gwyn's Island, roughly twenty miles from the mouth of the Rappahanock River. Leading a force of about twenty armed men in three boats, Wood attacked the 1,400-ton vessel, capturing it without any serious resistance. As with his first victim, he had the ship stripped and then fired. On 31 October, Wood and his raiders returned to Richmond with their spoils and several prisoners.[54] The Union Navy soon moved to counteract the activities of the Confederacy's "Horse Marine" and his navy on wheels. On 17 November, Gideon Welles, Lincoln's Secretary of the Navy, ordered the commander of the Potomac Flotilla to caution his fleet commanders about "the designs of the rebels to surprise and capture some [of] our steamers in the waters of Virginia."[55]

Wood was fast becoming one of the Confederacy's most prominent naval officers. On 9 February 1863, he received notification that effective 26 January he had been appointed naval aide-de-camp [ADC] to President Jefferson Davis, with the statutory rank and pay of Colonel of Cavalry in the Provisional Army.[56] His dual rank would permit him to provide liaison between the army and navy. That same day, Davis ordered Wood to "proceed to Wilmington, Charleston, Savannah, Mobile, Port Hudson, and Vicksburg for the purpose of inspection and report."[57] During the course of his tour of Southern ports, Wood carefully inspected naval defenses and ship construction, making recommendations directly to the president. "This occupied some months," he later recalled, "and while at Charleston and Vicksburg [I] was present at some of the operations around those places."[58] Perhaps the most significant outcome of Wood's tour was the strengthening of the defenses at Wilmington, North Carolina, where, he noted in a report to Davis, "the great want, the absolute necessity of the place if it is to be held against a naval attack, is heavy guns, larger caliber."[59] Partly as a result of Wood's recommendations, Wilmington managed to remain open as a blockade-running port until January 1865.[60]

Opposite: Wood (*lower right*) with other members of President Davis' staff (*Rise and Fall of the Confederate Government*).

Returning to Richmond in the spring of 1863, Wood soon began making plans for a second raiding expedition on Chesapeake Bay. Hoping this time to strike at enemy gunboats, he assembled a sizable force of seventy-one men and eleven officers. Accompanied by four boats on wagons, the raiders left Richmond on 12 August. Wood first established a base on the Piankatank River; however, an encounter with the enemy forced him to move his mobile naval force overland to the Rappahannock River, where they arrived on 19 August.[61]

After spending three nights unsuccessfully hunting for Federal vessels, on the early morning of 23 August the raiders discovered the gunboats USS *Satellite* and USS *Reliance* anchored near the mouth of the Rappahanock. Realizing that the two ships were "so close to each other that it was necessary to board both at the same time," Wood decided that he would lead the assault on the *Satellite*, while Lieutenant Frank L. Hoge would take charge of the boarding of the *Reliance*.[62] Both vessels would be attacked simultaneously by two boats, one on each bow. After Wood lead his men in prayer, his customary prelude to battle, the four Confederate boats moved forward. "It was," according to one of Wood's raiders, "a moment of anxiety — almost of misgiving. If the Yankees were aware of our approach, destruction was certain."[63] Once alongside the two Union vessels, the Confederate raiding parties rushed over the sides, cutting through the nettings that had been erected as a defense against boarders. Following some desperate hand-to-hand fighting, especially onboard the *Reliance*, the warships were captured and taken to Urbanna.[64]

After removing the Union and Confederate wounded and landing his prisoners, Wood arranged for a complement of sharpshooters to join the two captured Union vessels. He then divided the available coal between the two gunships and steamed back down the Rappahanock to resume raiding. It soon became apparent, however, that the *Reliance's* engines were malfunctioning, so the *Satellite* proceeded alone. Weather conditions in Chesapeake Bay were so bad that Wood was forced to abandon his hunt for prey until the night of 24 August, when he succeeded in capturing three merchant schooners, *Golden Rod*, *Coquette*, and *Two Brothers*. After towing the three vessels to Urbanna on 25 August, Wood took on coal and then returned once more to the bay; however, bad weather and the presence of several large Federal gunboats soon forced his retreat to Urbanna. The next day, Wood decided to take his prizes further upriver to evade pursuing Union warships. Before leaving, he was forced to strip and fire the *Golden Rod*, as her draft was too deep for the upper Rappahannock. Not long after his arrival upriver at Port Royal, Wood learned that a Union attack was imminent. As a result, the *Satellite, Reliance, Coquette,* and *Two Brothers* were also stripped and scuttled. During the operation, Wood's men exchanged cannon fire with the approaching Yankees.[65]

Wood's second Chesapeake raid was regarded as a triumph in the South, earning him considerable praise and attention. The *Richmond Sentinel* in particular lauded the "exceedingly handsome operation by Lieutenant Wood whose name is now famous ... Well done! Well done!"[66] As for the North, Wood's predations proved to be a major embarrassment to the Union Navy, which instituted a court of enquiry to investigate the loss of the *Satellite* and *Reliance.* At the same time, the commander of the Potomac Flotilla, Commodore Andrew Harwood, authorized a prolonged search for the elusive Wood.[67]

During the fall of 1863, Wood resumed his duties as an ADC in Richmond. In December, in recognition of his "gallant and meritorious conduct" in the Chesapeake expedition, he was promoted commander effective 23 August.[68] Not long after, he was called upon to assist Robert E. Lee in the planning of a combined operation designed to recapture New Bern, North Carolina, from the Federals. It was decided that the army forces would be led by General George Pickett, while Wood would support the land phase of the attack by seizing one or more enemy gunboats.[69]

Drawing from the crews of Confederate gunboats stationed at Wilmington, Richmond, and Charleston and making every effort to maintain secrecy, Wood assembled a force of thirty-three officers and 220 enlisted men, including twenty-five marines, all of whom rendezvoused at Kinston, North Carolina, on 31 January.[70] The three parties of raiders arrived by rail, bringing with them a total of fourteen boats: twelve cutters and two large launches armed with twelve-pounder howitzers. Upon their arrival, Wood ordered the men into their boats and sent them down the Neuse River to a small island below Kinston. After ensuring that the two larger boats would follow later, Wood joined his raiders and, for the first time, informed them that their objective was the boarding of enemy gunboats at New Bern. According to Donald B. Conrad, a surgeon who served on the expedition, Wood's announcement was met with an enthusiastic response: "It was a grand scheme, and was received by the older men with looks of admiration and with rapture by the young midshipmen, all of whom would have broken out into loud cheers but for the fact that the strictest silence was essential to the success of the daring undertaking."[71]

For the trip down the Neuse to New Bern, Wood divided his force into two groups. He took charge of one division and placed the other under Lieutenant Benjamin P. Loyall. With muffled oars the boats began their nighttime descent of the river. Midshipman J. Thomas Scharf described the journey: "Now the Neuse broadened until the boats seemed to be on a lake; again the tortuous stream narrowed until the party could almost touch the trees on either side ... No other sound was heard to break the stillness save the constant steady splash of the oars and the ceaseless surge of the river."[72] Arriving at New Bern in the early hours of 1 February, Wood was unable to locate a single Union warship. Just before daylight, he led his men a few miles back up the river to Batchelor's Creek, where they established a bivouac. The exhausted raiders would have to wait until nightfall before they could renew their search for prey. Meanwhile, the land forces under Pickett began their attack.[73]

After sunset, Wood and Loyall led a small party in search of Federal vessels. "We had not gone two miles," Loyall recounted, "when simultaneously we both cried 'There she is!' We discovered a black steamer anchored close up to the right flank of the outer fortifications of New Bern, where she had come that day."[74] Wood decided to attack the vessel that night, between midnight and 4:00 AM. He had chosen a formidable opponent: the USS *Underwriter*, a sidewheel steamer of 341 tons, with two 800-horsepower engines. Manned by a seasoned crew of twelve officers and seventy-two men, she was 186 feet long and carried a 20-pounder Parrott rifle and four 32-pounder Dahlgrens.[75]

Later that night Wood's force pulled down the Neuse River toward New Bern. As they neared their goal, he called the men together in prayer. For the raider Scharf, it was "a strange and ghostly sight, the men resting on their oars with heads uncovered, the commander also bareheaded, standing erect in the stern of his boat; the black waters rippling beneath."[76] At 2:00 AM the boats were ordered forward. One column, commanded by Wood, attacked forward; a second, under Loyall, struck aft. As they rapidly approached the looming hull of the ship, Wood and Loyall urged their men on: "Give way, boys, give way!"[77] Within moments, the Confederates, armed with pistols and cutlasses, scrambled over the side through a deadly hail of gunfire. The ensuing fight was described by Loyall as "furious, and at close quarters. Our men were eager, and as one would fall another came on. Not one faltered or fell back. The cracking of fire arms and the rattle of cutlasses made a deafening din."[78]

After about ten minutes of vicious hand-to-hand combat on the slippery, blood-covered deck, the boarders won control of the vessel. As his medical officer tended to the wounded (the raiders had sustained thirty casualties and the defenders twenty-seven), Wood quickly moved to escape with his prize. Much to his disappointment, he realized that he would have to scuttle the warship. Not only were her fires banked, but she soon came under bombardment from shore batteries. Wood ordered the wounded and the Confederate dead removed from the ship and his prisoners loaded. The vessel was then set ablaze. As they pulled away, the raiders "could hear now and then the boom of the guns of the *Underwriter* as they were discharged by heat." Then they heard "the awful explosion of the sturdy vessel, when fire reached her magazine."[79]

Even with the destruction of the *Underwriter*, Wood was confident that a combined assault utilizing his small boats would succeed in capturing New Bern; however, in the face of a faltering army attack, a cautious General Pickett eventually decided to withdraw, forcing Wood to reluctantly order his commandos back to Richmond.[80] Although Wood remained disappointed over the failure of the combined operation, others were quick to praise his role in the attack. Robert E. Lee, in his report on the operation, singled out Wood for praise: "Commander Wood who had the hardest part to perform did his part well."[81] On 15 February, the Confederate Congress unanimously passed a resolution formally thanking the Horse Marine not only for the capture of the *Underwriter* but for all of his commando operations, which were deemed "daring and brilliantly executed plans."[82]

Perhaps the greatest praise for Wood's part in the attack on New Bern came from the enemy. After the war, Union Admiral David Dixon Porter, commenting on the capture of the *Underwriter*, wrote: "This was a rather mortifying affair for the navy, however fearless on the part of the Confederates. This gallant expedition was led by Commander John Taylor Wood. It was to be expected that with so many clever officers, who left the Federal navy, and cast their fortunes with the Confederates, such gallant action would often be attempted."[83] Porter also agreed with Wood that a combined attack would likely have succeeded.

Despite the setback at New Bern, Davis and Lee were determined to regain control of the North Carolina sounds, and plans were soon underway for a second combined operation in the area. This time, the target would be Plymouth on the Roanoke River, and the land attack would be led by a more aggressive commander, Brigadier General Robert Hoke. Wood was once more placed in charge of the naval forces. The navy's role in the operation would be crucial, as Plymouth was protected not only by heavy fortifications, but also by a squadron of four gunboats: *Miami* (eight guns), *Southfield* (six guns), *Ceres* (four guns), and *Whitehead* (four guns). Confederate hopes for success rested with the ironclad CSS *Albemarle*, then in the final stages of construction at Edward's Ferry on the Roanoke River.[84]

Hoke launched his attack on the Union stronghold on 17 April. He had assumed that the *Albemarle* would shortly join the fray; however, as a result of various mishaps she was delayed until 19 April. In spite of her late arrival, the ironclad's intervention was decisive. After ramming and sinking the *Southfield*, she promptly drove off the remaining Federal gun-boats. Next she turned her big guns on the enemy's defenses. On the following day, Plymouth surrendered. In addition to nearly 3000 prisoners, the Confederates captured thirty pieces of artillery, a large stand of rifles, and substantial quantities of coal and stores. A jubilant Wood cabled the president: "Heaven has crowned our efforts with success."[85] After the capture of Plymouth, Hoke continued his campaign in eastern North Carolina, retaking Washington and threatening New Bern. However, just as he was on the verge of recapturing the latter center, he was ordered to Virginia, where the new Union commander, Lieutenant General Ulysses S. Grant, had launched a massive spring offensive.

The Federal campaign against the Army of Northern Virginia in May and June 1864 resulted in a series of bloody battles, beginning with the Wilderness, in northern Virginia, on 5 May. During this period Wood provided liaison between President Davis and various Confederate commanders.[86] In his capacity as ADC he was present at the last major battle of the Union offensive: Cold Harbor.[87] Here, on 3 June, the two armies met in a brutal engagement that saw Grant lose nearly 7,000 men in a suicidal charge which lasted less than ten minutes. Following the battle, the Federals withdrew southward to Petersburg, where, after several clashes, they began to dig in for a lengthy siege. The war was entering its final phase, and the desperate Confederate leadership became more willing to consider bold actions that could affect the upcoming elections in the Union and possibly bring about a just conclusion to the war. Not surprisingly, one of the most daring plans involved John Taylor Wood.

Early in July, Wood and another aide to the president, Robert E. Lee's son, Major-General G.W. Custis Lee, were given joint command of a combined operation designed to free several thousand Confederates imprisoned at Point Lookout, Maryland, located below Baltimore, at the mouth of Potomac.[88] Lee was placed in charge of the land forces, while Wood assumed responsibility for the naval forces. Their expedition against Point Lookout was timed to coincide with a planned invasion of Maryland and then Washington by the Army of the Valley led by Lieutenant General Jubal Early. It was hoped that the freed Confederates would bolster the attack on Washington.[89]

As Custis Lee coordinated the various elements of the land operation, Wood left for Wilmington, where he selected and fitted two steamers for the expedition, assembling crews "sufficiently large to capture any gun-boats at Point Lookout."[90] Meanwhile, Early's invasion of Maryland began on 5 July. Five days later, Wood's naval forces steamed down the Cape Fear River and were on the verge of running the blockade when they were forced to reverse their course. "At the last moment," Wood later wrote, "as we were crossing the bar at the mouth of the Cape Fear River, orders were telegraphed from Genl. Lee to return. He had received information that the enemy had notice of our designs."[91] On 11 July, Early reached the outskirts of Washington; however, the strength of the Union defenses soon forced a Confederate retreat across the Potomac. Although Wood was disappointed that the Point Lookout expedition had been compromised (most of the prisoners at the Union facility had been evacuated on 7 July) and that the invasion of Washington had failed, he was very soon presented with another opportunity to run the blockade and strike at the Yankee foe.

For some time Wood had been observing blockade runners that arrived in Wilmington, looking for a fast steamer that could be converted into a cruiser. On 15 July he finally found a suitable vessel: the *Atalanta*, a sleek, iron twin-screw powered by two 100-horsepower engines. Built on the Thames, at Millwall, below London, the ship displaced 700 gross tons and was 220 feet long, with a twenty-four-foot beam. Not long after her arrival in Wilmington on 15 July, she was acquired by the Confederate Navy and quickly armed with three guns: a rifled 100-pounder amidships, a rifled 32-pounder forward, and a long Parrott aft. Drawing her crew from the vessels of the James River Squadron and various gunboats stationed in North Carolina waters, the ship was commissioned as the CSS *Tallahassee* on 20 July 1864.[92] Three days later, Wood was formally named commander of the new raider. Although Wood's commission from the Confederate Secretary of the Navy, Stephen Mallory, allowed considerable leeway, it was clear that the *Tallahassee's* main objective was to attack Yankee shipping in the North's own coastal waters: "The character and force of your vessel point to the enemy's commerce as her most appropriate field of action, and it is hoped that her speed and capacity for carrying fuel will enable her to pay proper attention to the shores of New England and its fisheries."[93]

Following ten days of intensive drilling, Wood was satisfied that his vessel and her crew were ready. On 4 August, the *Tallahassee* dropped down the Cape Fear River to await favourable conditions for running the Union gauntlet. Wood intended to escape to sea through the New Inlet, the eastern entrance to Wilmington; however, after two unsuccessful attempts, on the nights of 4 and 5 August, he determined to try the western entrance, the Old Inlet, which was protected by Fort Caswell. On the night of 6 August, after nearly grounding in shoal water, the *Tallahassee* safely crossed the bar and raced through the inshore blockading squadron, passing between two warships that fired wildly at her in the darkness. "I did not return their fire," Wood later recalled, "for fear it would have shown our position, and I did not want our true character to be known, preferring that they should suppose us an ordinary blockade-runner."[94]

The *Tallahassee* was not out of danger yet. The fastest blockading ships patrolled offshore, searching for vessels that had escaped the inshore blockaders under the cover of darkness. During the next day Wood found himself chased by three Federal cruisers. Although the Confederate raider easily eluded these pursuers, as night fell she had a much closer call when she suddenly came upon a fourth Union warship. The Yankee vessel quickly opened fire when her signals were not answered. "The shells passed uncomfortably near," Wood wrote, "but in a half-hour we lost sight of each other in the darkness." The *Tallahassee* had finally run the inner and outer blockades and could now go on the offensive.[95]

On 11 August, following a few uneventful days, during which the Confederate warship spoke several foreign vessels, Wood made his first prize, the schooner *Sarah A. Boyce* of Boston. After the removal of her crew and their personal belongings, as well as the vessel's chronometers, charts, medicine chests, and some provisions, she was scuttled. Four more captures followed in quick succession: the pilot boat *James Funk* (which Wood used as a tender), the bark *Bay State*, and the brigs *Carrie Estelle* and *A. Richards*. Late in the day, Wood seized another prize, the schooner *Carroll*, which he bonded after receiving her captain's assurance that he would take on the *Tallahassee's* prisoners and land them at New York. Wood then ordered the bark and two brigs burned. Not long after, he made yet another capture, the pilot boat *William Bell*. This vessel was also put to the torch. Wood's main objective in seizing the two pilot boats had been to secure a pilot who would take the *Tallahassee* through Hell Gate into Long Island Sound, permitting the raider to attack New York City. Much to his regret, he could not find a pilot willing to help him realize his daring plans.[96]

The next day saw the raider and her tender resume their predations, capturing a total of six vessels: the schooners *Atlantic*, *Spokane*, and *R.E. Packer*; the bark *Suliote*; the brig *Billow*; and the ship *Adriatic*. The latter vessel, at 989 tons, was Wood's most significant capture; however, she almost proved to be his undoing. Ordered to heave to, the *Adriatic* collided with the *Tallahassee* aft, destroying the cruiser's mainmast and sweeping her decks clear, even carrying away her iron bulwark rail. According to the raider's surgeon, William Shepardson, the damage could have been much worse: "Being a very large ship, towering high above us, she would have inevitably sunk us had she struck amidships."[97] In addition to her cargo, the *Adriatic* carried one hundred and seventy passengers, mostly German emigrants, who were panic-stricken until they received assurances that their Confederate captors did not intend to harm them. After transferring the ship's passengers to the bark *Suliote*, which he bonded, Wood ordered the *Adriatic* fired. As darkness fell, the *Tallahassee* stood in for the Massachusetts coast. Not long after, Wood burned his tender, the *James Funk*. It was a decision that he later regretted: "It was a mistake, for I was authorized by the government to fit out any prize as a cruiser, and this one ought to have been sent along the eastern coast."[98]

Once in New England waters, the *Tallahassee* continued to wreak havoc, making nineteen captures from 13 to 17 August, as she moved up the coast and into the Bay of Fundy. Although most of her victims were relatively small schooners engaged in either fishing or the coastal trade, she also seized and scuttled the bark *Glenarvon* (789 tons) and the ship *James Littlefield* (547 tons). The destruction of the *Glenarvon*, a fine new vessel from Thomaston, Maine, touched Wood and his officers: "We watched the bark as she slowly settled, strake by strake, until her deck was awash, and then her stern sank gradually out of sight until she was in an upright position, and one mast after another disappeared with all sail set, sinking as quietly if human hands were lowering her into the depths." As for the *James Littlefield*, which was loaded with Welsh coal, it was hoped that her cargo could be used to replenish the *Tallahassee's* depleted fuel supply; however, the persistence of rough seas in the Bay of Fundy prohibited a safe transfer, forcing Wood to reluctantly leave "her to be a home for the cod and lobster."[99]

In need of fuel and repairs, on 18 August the *Tallahassee* abandoned her hunt for Yankee prey and steamed into the neutral port of Halifax, Nova Scotia, where Wood and his officers were warmly received by the Confederate agent Benjamin Wier and by the city's many Southern sympathizers, including Dr. William J. Almon, who took it upon himself to find a new mainmast for the warship.[100] Wood's official reception, though, was much less enthusiastic. By the summer of 1864, the likelihood of a Confederate victory had largely vanished, and as a consequence, British authorities were becoming increasingly unwilling to provoke the North.

Wood was especially taken aback by the treatment he received from the senior British naval officer, Vice-Admiral James Hope. "His manner and tone," the *Tallahassee's* commander reported, "were offensive."[101] The colony's lieutenant-governor, Richard Graves MacDonnell, was more cordial; however, partly as a result of concerted pressure from the vigilant American consul in Halifax, Judge Mortimer Jackson, MacDonnell went

The CSS *Tallahassee* in Halifax harbor, August 1864 [see note no. 100] (*from the Collection of the Maritime Museum of the Atlantic, N4959*).

to great lengths to ensure that the *Tallahassee* only loaded enough coal to permit her return to Wilmington. He was also insistent that the warship leave port after twenty-four hours, as required by British neutrality regulations. Nonetheless, once he was convinced that Wood intended to comply with his directives, the lieutenant-governor became more cooperative, acceding to the Confederate commander's request, on the afternoon of 19 August, for an additional half-day in port in order to permit the shipping of a mainmast.[102]

Despite the respite granted by MacDonnell, Wood had no intention of remaining in Halifax for any longer than was necessary. During his brief stay in the Nova Scotian capital, he had received intelligence indicating that Union warships had been sighted just off the harbor's entrance. Determined to avoid capture, Wood had carefully studied a chart of Halifax harbor and had decided to leave before the *Tallahassee's* new mainmast was shipped, taking his cruiser out through the Eastern Passage, a narrow channel used only by small, local craft.[103] Late that night, with the assistance of Jock Flemming, an experienced local pilot supplied by Benjamin Wier, the *Tallahassee* used her twin-screw engines to advantage, gingerly navigating the sharp twists and turns of the Eastern Passage and slipping out of port. "Soon we felt the pulsating bosom of the old Atlantic," wrote Wood, "and were safe outside, leaving our waiting friends miles to the westward."[104]

Although it now appears unlikely that any Federal warships were actually lurking outside the harbor at the time of Wood's departure, the *Tallahassee's* nighttime voyage through Halifax's dangerous Eastern Passage stands as a bold feat of navigation by one of the Confederacy's most fearless naval commanders.[105] Certainly Wood remained forever grateful to the pilot Flemming. "Years afterwards," he later wrote, "I would meet the old man and over a glass of beer at Capt. Bird's he would love to talk of taking the *Tallahassee* out the Eastern Passage the darkest night he ever saw. Let him R.I.P."[106]

The *Tallahassee's* return voyage was largely uneventful. In fact, during the six-day trip she only made a single capture: the brig *Roan*. Wood had hoped to steam to Bermuda in order to obtain the coal required to continue his cruise; however, an outbreak of Yellow Jack on the island forced him to head for the *Tallahassee's* home port of Wilmington. On 25 August, the cruiser approached the North Carolina coast, entering what Wood described as "troubled waters." During the day the *Tallahassee* was chased by two of the outlying blockaders. Wood managed to elude these pursuers, and as darkness fell, the *Tallahassee* ran in toward Masonboro Inlet. As she neared Fort Fisher, the raider found her way blocked by the USS *Monticello*, which was positioned close to shore, almost in the surf. Sheering away, Wood quickly moved to sweep around the Federal warship on the seaward side. The *Monticello* then opened fire on what she assumed was a blockade runner. Much to the Federals' surprise, the Confederate cruiser replied in kind. Soon other Union warships joined the fray. As a confused and ineffectual cannonade punctured the darkness around him, Wood cooly steamed through the Federal vessels and signaled Fort Fisher. "A few minutes later the range lights were set," he recalled, "and by their guidance, we safely crossed the bar and anchored close under the fort."[107] According to William Shepardson, Wood then called all hands to muster and "read prayers, thanking God for having protected us through scenes of peril, and for delivering us from the hands of our enemies, bringing us safe into our destined port."[108]

Wood, who had already achieved considerable renown as the Confederacy's "Horse Marine," saw his fame increase as a result of his exploits as the commander of the *Tallahassee*. This new acclaim was manifested in a variety of ways, including the naming of Battery Wood on the James River in his honor and the publication of naval songwriter E. King's "A Song for the Forecastle," dedicated to the crew of the *Tallahassee*.[109] Mary Boykin Chesnut, who had entertained Wood at her salons in Richmond, probably reflected the general Southern pride in his accomplishments when she noted in her famous diary: "John Taylor Wood, fine fellow, in his fine ship *Tallahassee*. He is all right."[110] Such recognition was a fitting response to Wood's achievement. In the space of only nineteen days, the *Tallahassee* had made more captures than any other Confederate raider in 1864. In fact, only three Confederate warships had more successful overall careers: CSS *Alabama*, CSS *Florida*, and CSS *Shenandoah*. Unlike those vessels, however, Wood's cruiser had been outfitted and equipped in the South and had been manned with CSN officers and crew. Furthermore, she had sailed from, and had returned to, a Confederate port. (For these reasons, Wood would later resent the fact that his raider was implicated in the post-war Alabama Claims.)[111] Jefferson Davis would later summarize the *Tallahassee's* cruise as "brief, but brilliant while it lasted."[112]

Not everyone in the South, however, looked favourably upon the *Tallahassee's* predations. Although her successes against Yankee shipping raised morale at a time when the South was experiencing serious reverses, they also resulted in a tightening of the blockade around Wilmington, the Confederacy's most important lifeline. Among those concerned about the repercussions of the raider's cruise was Robert E. Lee, who expressed his misgivings in a letter to Secretary of War James A. Seddon on 24 September: "The question arises, whether it is more important to us to obtain supplies through that port or to prey upon the enemy's commerce by privateers sent from there."[113]

An even more vocal opponent of the raider's activities was the governor of North Carolina, Zebulon Vance, who wrote to Jefferson Davis on 14 October, requesting that the *Tallahassee* and her sister ship, the *Chickamauga*, refrain from further cruising and be utilized, instead, to strengthen the defense of Wilmington.[114] Vance's letter prompted Stephen Mallory to send a spirited defense of the two raiders to Davis on 22 October. Mindful of the need for a forceful but tactful reply to Vance, Davis assigned the file to Wood, who had returned to his duties as a presidential aide in early September.[115] In the letter that he subsequently drafted for Davis, Wood drew upon Mallory's text to offer a strong defense of his own cruise as well as rationale for further cruising: "Though the *Tallahassee* captured 31 vessels, her service is not measured by, nor limited to, the value of these ships and cargoes and the number of her prisoners, but it must be estimated in connection with other results; the consequent insecurity of the United States coastwise commerce, the detention and delay of vessels in port, and the augmentation of the rate of marine insurance, by which millions were added to the expense of navigation, and the compulsory withdrawal of the blockading force from Wilmington in pursuit of her."[116]

Obviously, Wood, Davis, and Mallory were all of one mind on the issue; so it is not surprising that the *Tallahassee*, renamed CSS *Olustee*, made a second cruise, in November, before being converted into the government blockade runner *Chameleon*, under the command of Wood's future business partner, John Wilkinson. Interestingly, Wilkinson was a bitter critic of the activities of the Wilmington-based commerce-destroyers and of what he termed the "official imbecility" of Stephen Mallory's policies regarding the Confederate cruisers.[117]

In the months following the *Tallahassee's* cruise, Wood, as Jefferson Davis's ADC, was increasingly involved in the efforts to protect Richmond and break Grant's siege of Petersburg. He later offered the following curt summary of this part of his career: "With the President and Genl. Lee took part in the fights around Richmond."[118] This likely means that he was present at least some of the battles that marked the latter stages of the Petersburg Campaign. During this period Wood also re-established contact with his friend William Hewett, a British naval officer and Victoria Cross-winner who had witnessed the fight between the *Virginia* and the *Monitor* and who had later become a noted blockade runner. Not long after the *Tallahassee's* return voyage, Hewett likewise steamed from Halifax for Wilmington, but his ship, the *Condor*, ran aground off Fort Fisher on 1 October 1864, resulting in the death of the Confederate spy Rose O'Neal Greenhow. "Later," Wood wrote, "I convoyed him through General Grant's lines to Richmond, doing a little skirmishing together."[119] After the war, Hewett resumed his naval career, eventually becoming a Vice-Admiral in the British Navy.

Late in January 1865, Wood participated in his last naval battle. The withdrawal of many Federal vessels from the James to bolster the assault on Fort Fisher provided CSN Secretary Mallory with a long-awaited opportunity to send the James River Squadron downstream to attack Grant's base at City Point and thereby break the siege of Petersburg. The prospects for success seemed encouraging. The squadron could pit three heavy ironclads, CSS *Richmond*, CSS *Virginia II*, and CSS *Fredericksburg*, against the reduced Union naval forces, which then included only one ironclad, the monitor USS *Onondaga*. However, the capital navy was severely hampered by the inaction of its cautious commander, Commodore John K. Mitchell.[120] Starting on 16 January, Mallory repeatedly urged Mitchell to pass the Union obstructions at Trent's Reach and attack City Point; all to no avail. Five days later, the frustrated Secretary dispatched John Taylor Wood to assist Mitchell in the planning of the attack and to provide the James River Squadron with some aggressive leadership.[121] Finally, on the evening of 23 January, the squadron moved down the river.

Even with the participation of Wood and other bold commanders, such as Charles Read, John McIntosh Kell, and Robert D. Minor, the ensuing engagement proved to be a fiasco for the Confederates. That night, as the squadron attempted to pass the obstructions at Trent's Reach, four vessels, the ironclads *Virginia II* and *Richmond*, the torpedo boat *Scorpion*, and the gunboat *Drewry*, all grounded. On the morning of 24 January the stranded vessels came under punishing fire, first from Federal shore batteries and later from the big guns of the *Onondaga*. Union gunners destroyed the *Drewry* and incapacitated the *Scorpion*, which was later captured. They also inflicted serious damage on the *Virginia II* before she was able to float free and proceed upstream with the *Richmond* and the other remaining vessels of the James River Squadron.[122]

As the Confederates licked their wounds under the guns of Battery Dantzler (just below Battery Wood), Mitchell decided that the squadron should make a second attempt to pass the Union obstructions that night. However, when the Confederates returned to Trent's Reach, it quickly became apparent that Union defenses (including the use of a blinding spotlight) and the poor condition of the squadron's vessels precluded a successful descent of the James. Following a council of war, the hapless Confederates retreated upriver. For Secretary Mallory, the blame for the debacle at Trent's Reach could be laid squarely on the shoulders of the James River Squadron's commander, and he quickly moved to replace Mitchell with a more able and daring officer. His first choice was Wood, but the presidential aide, realizing, perhaps, that the CSN had largely ceased to be a factor in the war, declined.[123] Mallory then approached Raphael Semmes, who assumed command of the squadron on 18 February.

Not long after Wood refused the command of the James River Squadron, his contributions to the Confederacy were honored in another way. On 10 February he was promoted Post Captain, in recognition of the capture of the *Underwriter* and for the cruise of the *Tallahassee*.[124] He was not destined to serve long with his new rank. On Sunday morning, 2 April, as he sat with Jefferson Davis in St. Paul's Church in Richmond, a telegram arrived from Robert E. Lee, announcing that the Confederate lines at Petersburg had broken and that the government would have to immediately evacuate the capital. After quickly packing his own belongings, Wood spent the day boxing the presidential archives. That night he and Davis boarded a train, which would carry the members of the Confederate government to Danville, Virginia, where Davis hoped to establish a new capital. During the evacuation of Richmond, the James River Squadron was blown up, the bridges over the James were destroyed, and the city's warehouses were fired. Soon, the resulting fires were burning out of control and much of the capital was engulfed in flames.[125]

Chapter 5

Escape to Cuba, 1865

On 3 April, the day that Wood and the other members of the Confederacy's leadership disembarked at Danville, Abraham Lincoln arrived in Petersburg. The following day, the U.S. president toured the smoldering ruins of Richmond and is even reputed to have visited Davis's study, sitting at the recently abandoned desk of his Southern foe. With the capital in Yankee hands, the Confederate dream of independence was fast becoming the Lost Cause, although Davis persisted in the desperate hope that the unequal struggle would somehow continue.

During the next few days in Danville, Wood worked on Davis' papers and helped the president establish an office.[126] On 8 April, the exhausted ADC was granted two day's leave, allowing him to travel by train to Greensboro, North Carolina, where his wife and children had taken refuge. Just as he was about to return to Virginia, on 10 April, Wood received word that General Lee had surrendered at Appomattox and that the president and cabinet were on their way south to Greensboro.[127] Davis and the other Confederate leaders were not warmly received by the people of North Carolina. In fact, most of the cabinet members were forced to take up quarters in a railroad car. The president was obliged to move in with Wood.

On 12 April, as Davis was discussing the possibility of continuing the war, he finally received official confirmation of Lee's surrender. Lee's son Robert later described the scene in Wood's lodgings as Davis read General Lee's dispatch: "After reading it, he handed it without comment to us; then, turning away, he silently wept bitter tears. He seemed quite broken at the moment by this tangible evidence of the loss of his army and the misfortune of its general. All, of us, respecting his great grief, silently withdrew, leaving him with Colonel Wood."[128] As Wood comforted his uncle, he must have wondered about his own fate and the future of his family.

Wood's uncle, CSA President Jefferson Davis (*Rise and Fall of the Confederate Government*).

Later that day he confided in his diary: "I can hardly realize this overwhelming disaster, it crushes the hopes of nearly all."[129]

On the following day, the Confederate cabinet held a council of war in Wood's quarters. During the course of this meeting, which Wood attended, Davis reluctantly agreed that his crumbling government had no choice but to authorize General Joseph E. Johnston to negotiate peace terms with Union General William T. Sherman. On 14 April, the day that John Wilkes Booth shot President Abraham Lincoln, Davis and his staff prepared to leave Greensboro, in flight from advancing Federal troops. The next day, Wood bid farewell to his family and rode southward with the president's party. Some of the Confederate refugees traveled in wagons; others, like Wood, were on horseback.[130]

During the next few days, Davis's entourage traveled south to Salisbury and then on to Charlotte, North Carolina, where, on 19 April, they learned of the death of Lincoln and of the fall of Mobile and Columbus. The president's party remained in Charlotte for nearly a week, awaiting word of the peace negotiations with Sherman. While in Charlotte, Davis, with Wood at his side, persisted in his futile efforts to sustain his government's will to continue the struggle for Southern independence. On 22 April, the Confederate leaders were informed that the Federals had rejected their peace terms. Four days later, General Johnston, Davis' best hope for continued resistance, surrendered to Sherman. Davis quickly prepared to head further south. A discouraged Wood reflected on the rapidly deteriorating situation that now confronted the president's party: "So we are falling to pieces."[131]

Pushing on into South Carolina, the refugees traveled to Cokesbury and then Abbeville, where they arrived on 2 May. Here, Davis held a final, pathetic council of war, during which it became apparent even to him that the war was lost and that the Confederate government was no more. In the aftermath of this meeting, Wood and other aides quickly sorted through the president's papers, destroying a good deal of routine material, but preserving, in Wood's words, "records as would likely be of value in recording the life of the Confederacy." At the same time, the Confederate treasure was loaded on to wagons. At midnight, the party resumed its journey southward, reaching Washington, Georgia, on 3 May.[132]

After finding shelter in a local bank, Davis presided over his last official meeting as president. In preparation for his continued flight southward, he arranged for the disposition of the Confederate treasure and dismissed most of his cavalry escort. His smaller party, which now included only one Cabinet member, Postmaster General John H. Reagan, then resumed the journey south through Georgia. According to Wood, they traveled "incog. as returning soldiers. The P. [President] as a Texas member of Congress & Judge R. [Reagan] as a Texas Judge." On 5 May, in an effort to avoid capture, the group split into two parties. Even with this precaution, the possibility of escape was becoming increasingly remote. Not only had Confederate military resistance collapsed, but there was a sizeable reward being offered for Davis' capture. Furthermore, it had been widely reported that the Confederate leaders were fleeing with huge amounts of specie.[133]

The probability of capture became a virtual certainty on the night of 6 May, when Davis rushed to the aid of his wife, Varina Davis, who was traveling in a larger, separate entourage that had been threatened by marauding Union soldiers. As the combined Davis parties resumed their flight during the next few days, Federal forces in the area closed in. The evening of 9 May saw the presidential party camped just north of Irwinville, Georgia. Before dawn on the following day, two different Union cavalry detachments descended on the camp. In the darkness, the Federals mistook each other for enemy forces and opened fire. Roused by the sound of battle, the president's party scrambled to escape. Wood managed to reach Davis' tent and urged Varina Davis to hide with her husband in a nearby swamp. Prompted, according to Wood, by Varina Davis' extreme distress, the president quickly improvised a disguise, utilizing a waterproof and a shawl that belonged to his wife; however, these efforts to elude capture proved futile. Within moments Davis was surrounded and forced to reveal himself. Wood, who witnessed the capture, was distressed by his uncle's unmanly attire: "This attempted escape in disguise I regret exceedingly."[134] Later, Confederate commentators would vehemently deny that Davis was wearing women's clothing at the time of his capture. John H. Reagan, who most certainly knew better, characterized the charge as a "despicable slander."[135]

Shortly after Davis' capture, Wood obtained permission from his uncle to attempt an escape. The Confederate president well understood his nephew's reluctance to submit to Yankee authority without a fight. "His daring exploits on the sea," Davis later wrote, "had made him, on the part of the Federal Government, an object of special hostility."[136] Wood's hopes for escape were considerably bolstered by the fact that most of the Union captors seemed far more intent on looting than securing their Confederate prisoners. Accordingly, Wood tried to bribe his guard, a recent German immigrant who spoke little English. Offering the trooper a twenty-dollar gold piece, Wood used sign language to convince the German to escort him to a nearby stream and adjoining swamp. Once they were outside the camp and safely beyond the Union picket line, Wood paid the guard another twenty dollars to leave him at the stream. As the soldier left, Wood crept into the swamp and hid from view. Here he lay for almost three hours, often within a few yards of Union soldiers who came to water their horses. Not long after the Federals and their prisoners left the camp, Wood discovered a fellow escapee, Lieutenant Barnwell, a cavalry officer who had found two abandoned horses. Returning to the site of their earlier capture, Wood and Barnwell managed to scrounge enough material to outfit the two horses. Wood also found a derringer that had probably been dropped by Davis or Reagan, perhaps for Wood's benefit. He and Barnwell then headed south, spending the night at Widow Paulk's, about ten miles distant. Wood, who now passed himself off as a paroled soldier, was entering a loosely organized "underground passage" which offered him and other fleeing Confederates a glimmer of hope in their efforts to escape from the newly conquered South.[137]

On the following day, Wood and Barnwell resumed their journey southward, heading for the home of Barnwell's uncle outside Valdosta, Georgia. During their first day on the road, they encountered Judah P. Benjamin, the former Confederate Secretary of State, who was traveling under the alias Monsieur Bonfals. Wood and Benjamin agreed to attempt a rendezvous near Madison, Florida. On 13 May, Wood and Barnwell arrived at the home of Osbert Barnwell. After resting for two days, Wood left on his own for Madison, where, on 16 May, at General Joseph J. Finegan's home, he met General John C. Breckenridge, the Confederacy's last

Secretary of War — and a former U.S. vice-president. Like Wood, Breckenridge was determined to escape by way of Florida. After consulting with Finegan, Wood was convinced that the best hope for escape was by small boat from the east coast of Florida to the Bahamas. In deference to Wood's seamanship, Breckinridge concurred. Later that day, the fugitives left Madison, riding south across the Suwannee River and then along the old Augustine Road towards Gainesville. In addition to Wood and Breckinridge, their small party included Breckinridge's aide, Colonel James Wilson, and a black servant, Thomas Ferguson.[138]

Wood and Breckinridge's party reached Gainesville on 18 May. The following day, at the home of Congressman James B. Dawkins, they conferred with Captain J.J. Dickison, the Swamp Fox of the Confederacy, who, like Wood, had won renown for his wartime commando operations. Dickison heartily supported Wood's plan to attempt an escape from Florida's east coast. More importantly, Dickison offered the fugitives a lifeboat which he had retained from the USS *Columbine*, a Federal gunboat that he had captured and destroyed on the St. John's River in May 1864. As Dickison arranged for the boat to be prepared, Wood rode southwest alone to the plantation of former senator David Yulee, where he hoped to find Judah Benjamin, but the latter "was too wily to be found at the house of a friend." Wood then rejoined Breckinridge's party, which had moved on to Millwood Plantation, the home of Colonel Sam Owens. Here the fugitives met again with Dickison, who confirmed that their boat would shortly be ready at Fort Butler on the St. John's River. Dickison also provided them with a revolver and with a guide, Lieutenant William H. McCardell. During the next few days, the party traveled from one plantation to another, safely making their way to the St. John's River.[139]

On 26 May, they finally arrived at Fort Butler, where they found the lifeboat that Dickison had promised, as well as two paroled soldiers from his command, Sergeant Joseph O'Toole and Corporal Richard R. Russell, who offered their services to the fugitives (a third soldier, Private Murphy, also joined the party for a few days). The *Columbine's* boat proved to be a four-oared gig with little freeboard, about seventeen or eighteen feet long. If conditions were favorable, she could step a small mast. As the fugitives loaded the boat, her shortcomings quickly became apparent. "With our stores, arms, etc.," Wood observed, "it was a tight fit to get into the boat; there was no room to lie down or stretch." Nevertheless, the Yankee gig offered the promise of freedom, and it was with a sense of anticipation that the party soon embarked on their voyage down the St. John's River. "That night," Wood recalled, "we landed, like old campaigners, and were soon comfortable." However, the enthusiasm of Wood and his fellow fugitives was dampened later that night by a torrential downpour that soaked not only them, but a large portion of their supplies.[140]

The next morning, bolstered by a little rum, the members of the party were able to regain their good spirits. Over the course of the next two days, they passed down the deserted banks of the St. John's River to its head-waters, where it formed lakes Monroe and Harvey. During their cramped passage, the fugitives were ever mindful of alligators, which were plenti-ful in the river. "Occasionally," Wood wrote, " as we passed uncomfort-ably near, we could not resist, even with our scant supply of ammunition, giving them a little cold lead between the head and shoulder, the only vul-nerable place." On 28 May, the party crossed Lake Monroe. From this point on, the river became increasingly difficult for the overloaded gig to navigate. As a result, it was decided to make a portage of nearly thirty miles to the Indian River, an inland waterway extending along the eastern coast of Florida from Key Biscayne to Cape Canaveral and separated from the Atlantic Ocean only by a narrow sand ridge.[141]

On 29 May, at the mouth of Lake Harney, the party rendezvoused with a local tender whom Wood and O'Toole had hired to haul the lifeboat in a cart powered by a team of bulls. The overland trek, which took two days, proved to be an ordeal. Not only were the tender's bulls exceedingly uncooperative, but the heat was intense and the party was plagued by sand flies during the day and by mosquitoes at night. Wood later concluded that "It would have been less labor to have tied the beasts, put them into the boat, and hauled it across the portage." It was with a considerable sense of relief, then, that the party reached the Indian River on the following day. After making some minor repairs to their boat, they had to drag it out nearly half a mile through the river's shoal waters before they could embark on the next leg of their journey. It was with some trepidation that they began their voyage down the Indian River. While the nearby Atlantic beckoned, the possibility of capture also increased, as they were now in waters frequented by Federal forces.[142]

As they continued down the Indian River toward Jupiter Inlet, where they hoped to enter the Atlantic, the party generally made good progress. However, during those periods when the breeze died, they found the heat stifling. They were also tormented by swarms of mosquitoes and other insects. Nights were especially bad. "When sleeping on shore," Wood recounted, "the best protection was to bury ourselves in the sand, with cap drawn over the head (my buckskin gauntlets proved invaluable); if in the boat, to wrap the sail or tarpaulin around us." On the night of 2 June, the fugitives ran by the Union blockade station at Indian River Inlet, near Fort Pierce. On the following day, as they found themselves lost in Juniper

Narrows, a maze of narrow channels, swamps, and bayous, they had the good fortune to stumble on a short haulover to the Atlantic. After lugging their boat for about half a mile over sand dunes, the party reached the ocean. It was a welcome sight. They were now even closer to freedom, but also, of course, to possible capture.[143]

Sailing down the coast, the fugitives carefully watched for signs of Federal vessels. That night they anxiously passed Jupiter Inlet, where Wood expected to find another Union blockade station. The next morning they landed near the site of present-day Palm Beach. Here they obtained fresh water and bolstered their depleted provisions by foraging for turtles' eggs. As they awaited a favorable wind that would permit them to embark on their treacherous crossing, the fugitives took the opportunity to rest. Late in the day, as the sun set, they set out for the Bahamas. As was the case with his many wartime raiding expeditions, Wood began the voyage by reading a prayer. Probably more than anyone else in the party, the veteran mariner knew how improbable it was that they would actually reach Nassau in a small, open boat.[144]

Wood's apprehensions probably only increased that night as the gig struggled against a strong headwind, making virtually no progress. To make matters worse, on the morning of 5 June, he and his party were alarmed to spy an approaching steamer cruising very close to shore. Quickly landing, the fugitives scrambled to pull their boat well up on the sand dunes, where it would hopefully blend in with the beach flotsam and jetsam. They then hid behind a dune and watched the Federal vessel. Much to their relief, the cruiser passed them by, and they soon left their hiding place and were preparing to relaunch their boat, when they realized that the steamer had turned about. It was obvious to Wood that a sharp lookout had spied the Confederates on the beach.

While Breckinridge and his aide, Wilson, recommended that the party flee into the bush that bordered the beach, Wood was loath to abandon their boat and proposed a bolder response: he and the two paroled soldiers, Russell and O'Toole, would row out to meet the Federals, who were in the process of launching a small boat. Ever the resourceful commando, Wood was confident that he could bluff his way out of the situation. As he and his two boatmates pulled towards the approaching Federal cutter, he was encouraged by the discovery that "The sheen was not yet off the lace and buttons of the youngster in charge." The wily Wood was not only able to convince the inexperienced Union captain that the Confederates were paroled soldiers returning home, but he also was able to arrange for a trade of turtle eggs for some plug tobacco. As the cutter pulled away, the Federal ships's coxswain informed the young officer that Wood's boat looked suspiciously like a man-of-war's gig. Fortunately for the Confederates, the youngster paid no attention.[145]

While the fugitives had managed to avoid capture, they soon discovered that the sharp headwind precluded any possibility of their attempting another crossing to the Bahamas. Consequently, they were forced to continue further down the Florida coastline, which probably meant that their next attempt would be a crossing to Cuba. On the morning of 6 June, they encountered a small encampment of Seminole Indians, where they were warmly received. After partaking of a meal of *koonti* and fish, the Confederates completed a trade, reluctantly parting with some of their gunpowder in exchange for a supply of *koonti*. "We parted good friends, after smoking the pipe of piece," Wood later recollected. During this encounter, Wood likely reflected on his own childhood years in Florida and on the role his family had played in the decimation of the Seminole nation.[146]

Later that day, south of Lake Worth, the fugitives spotted a sail standing to the northward. At first they were alarmed, but as the stranger maneuvered to avoid them, they quickly surmised that it was likely manned by deserters and that it was a larger and more seaworthy craft, one that offered a far better chance of making the dangerous voyage to Cuba. Led by one of the Confederacy's greatest sea raiders, the Confederates quickly downed their sail, manned their oars, and gave chase. After a short pursuit, a shot from the Confederates finally convinced the deserters to drop their mainsail. Once the Confederates were alongside, Wood and Breckinridge stepped into the larger boat with revolvers drawn. Although the deserters were themselves armed, they were intimidated by the fierce-looking and desperate Confederates and eventually agreed to an exchange of boats. Wood was very pleased with his final capture of the war: "sloop-rigged, not much longer than our gig, but with more beam and plenty of free-board, decked over to the mast, and well found in sails and rigging. After our experience in a boat the gunwale of which was not more than eighteen inches out of the water, we felt that we had a craft able to cross the Atlantic."[147]

While a voyage to Cuba now seemed more realistic, it was essential that the fugitives find adequate provisions. For this reason, they sailed up the Miami River to Fort Dallas (now Miami), where, amidst the ruins of an abandoned Seminole War fort, a trading post had been established. Wood and his party approached the post with the utmost caution, as it was a known refuge for wreckers, deserters, and other outlaws. The Confederates' wariness only increased as their sloop neared the trading-post wharf, which was crowded with more than twenty armed men. "[A] more motley and villainous crew never trod the deck of one of Captain Kidd's ships," observed Wood, who was determined not to trust their boat "within a hundred yards of the shore." Led by Wood, the Confederates endeavored to negotiate with the renegades. However, once it became apparent that the fugitives could not arrive at an arrangement that would guarantee their safety, Wood decided that the best course of action was to withdraw down the Miami River.[148]

As the small party moved away, the renegades pursued them in four or five canoes. The Confederates quickly prepared for action. "Although outnumbered three to one," Wood wrote, "still we were well under cover in our boat, and could rake each canoe as it came up." After two of the pursuers were hit and a canoe nearly overturned, hostilities ceased, and the renegades agreed to permit the soldier O'Toole to return to the post for provisions. Wood and his fellow fugitives were convinced that the renegades were likely awaiting the return of a larger boat, so it was decided that O'Toole should complete this transaction within two hours. After waiting for the allotted time — and then some — the Confederates reluctantly raised anchor and slowly departed from Fort Dallas. Not long after, they were relieved to spy a canoe astern and heaved to, awaiting its approach. It was O'Toole, accompanied by two renegades and a welcome supply of provisions, including a keg of rum. The Confederates then continued on their way. As night fell they anchored in Key Biscayne, where, according to Wood, they "passed an unhappy night fighting mosquitos."[149]

At dawn the next day, the Confederates were alarmed to sight a schooner to the eastwards. This unidentified vessel, which likely belonged either to the Federals or, as Wood assumed, to the Fort Dallas renegades, was in fast pursuit of the fugitives. Wood promptly took evasive action, maneuvring the sloop into shoal water and ordering all ballast overboard. Soon finding their passage blocked by a reef, the Confederates jumped overboard and worked the boat over the coral until they could move it no further. They now had no choice but to jettison anything in the sloop that was dispensable, including most of the provisions that had been obtained with such difficulty at Fort Dallas. Then the fugitives, three on each side, lifted the boat forward, struggling to find purchase on the treacherous reef. Although they kept all sail on, and were thus aided by the wind, they had to struggle for more than one hundred yards before they succeeded in clearing the reef and reaching deeper water. Even then, the sore and exhausted Confederates were not out of danger. As the fugitives left the shoal, their pursuers fired wildly with a nine- or twelve-pounder. Then, much to the Confederates' surprise, the schooner slipped through a channel in the reef and resumed the chase. Separated from the sloop by yet another reef, the schooner opened fire again, this time more accurately and with both a boat gun and small arms. Fortunately for the fugitives, shortly thereafter they discovered a break in the reef and were able to elude their determined pursuers.[150]

The Confederates soon reached Elliotts Key, where, amidst swarms of mosquitoes, they attempted to sleep. Later, they attended to their most pressing problem: the need for ballast. They also searched for additional provisions, with little success. Then resuming their voyage southward, they finally arrived at Caesar's Creek, a fast-flowing, crooked channel, with numerous inlets, that led to the ocean. After considerable difficulty, on the evening of 8 June they cleared the keys and threaded their way through a myriad of outlying reefs. At 10 PM the Confederates were abeam Carysfort Light opposite Key Largo, which receded into the distance as they sailed out into the dangerous waters of the Gulf Stream. The fugitives were now about to embark on the most treacherous leg of their journey. They likely took some solace from the fact that at the helm of their small craft was John Taylor Wood, one of America's greatest sailors. As for Wood himself, he was all too aware of what he and his fellow Confederates "might expect from summer squalls in the straits of Florida."[151]

Wood's apprehensions were well founded. Not long after they left the Florida coast, the fugitives encountered a vicious storm that struck, in his words, "with the force of a thunderbolt." As gale-force winds drove the little sloop through the pitching seas and torrential rains, Wood clung desperately to the tiller. Drawing upon his considerable skills as a seaman, Wood was able to ride out a series of fierce squalls; however, he became increasingly concerned about the threat of nearby reefs, and eventually decided that the sloop would have to heave to, an extremely dangerous maneuver under the circumstances. Passing the helm to Colonel Wilson, Wood loosened the mainsail and made a leg-of-mutton sail. Wood then ordered Wilson to put the helm a-starboard and let the sloop come to on the port tack as Wood hoisted the sail. All went well until Wood was securing the halyards, at which time the inexperienced Wilson gave too much helm, thus bringing the wind on the other bow and forcing the boom to fly around and knock Wood overboard. Fortunately for the other fugitives, who were all landlubbers, Wood was able to seize hold of the sheet and, with the assistance of General Breckinridge, regain the boat. Wood quickly returned to his position at the tiller. "For twelve hours, or more," he later recalled, "I did not trust the helm to any one."[152]

Later, the seas moderated sufficiently to give the Confederates some respite; however, their rations were now alarmingly low and, to make matters worse, they were beginning to suffer from exposure. Fortunately, they were eventually able to hail an American vessel, the brig *Neptune,* from Bangor, Maine. The brig's captain was extremely wary of the fugitives, but he did provide them with some much-needed water as well as a large bag of hardtack biscuits. Wood could well appreciate the Yankee master's less-than-enthusiastic reception of the sloop and its occupants: "when the time and place are considered, we cannot wonder at the captain's precautions, for a more piratical-looking party than we never sailed the Spanish Main."[153]

On 10 June the fugitives were elated to sight some rocky inlets that Wood recognized as Doubleheaded Shot Keys. This meant that they were now outside American waters and on the edge of Salt Key Bank, approaching the coast of Cuba. As they crossed the crystal-clear waters of the bank, the Confederates were so tantalized by the panorama of marine life below their boat that the soldier Russell was prompted to dive for shellfish to feed his boat mates. That night, the fugitives spied a lighthouse, an indication that they had nearly reached asylum. After sailing westward for several hours along the Cuban coast, they approached a large town at the head of a bay. It was now the morning of 11 June. At General Breckinridge's urging, Wood led the men in prayer, offering thanks for their "wonderful escape." For the Confederate naval veteran, this heartfelt supplication marked the end of a long and desperate journey to freedom that had begun just over one month before, on 10 May, the day of his uncle's humiliating capture. And while Wood's survival through the ordeal certainly owed much to providence, it was also attributable to his own extraordinary resourcefulness and seamanship.[154]

Wood shortly after his arrival in British North America, 1865 (*The Century Illustrated Monthly Magazine*).

Following prayers, Wood anchored close to the town's custom house and signaled to the shore. When it became apparent that no one was being dispatched to receive the sloop, Wood went ashore and reported to the local customs officials, who informed him that he had arrived at Cardenas, a small city on Cuba's northern coast, some seventy-five miles from Havana. Initially, the Cardenas authorities greeted Wood and his boat mates with considerable caution, telegraphing the Spanish governor general in Havana for instructions. However, once the Cubans realized that the boat's occupants were senior Confederate officials, the fugitives were accorded a decidedly warmer reception. Soon their sturdy little sloop was registered under *No Name,* and the exhausted and hungry men were permitted to land and partake of the hospitality of Cardenas' sizeable colony of Southerners. An appreciative Wood later marveled at the "transition from a small boat at sea, naked and starving, to the luxuries and comforts of civilized life." That night he and his fellow Confederates were feted at a large banquet.[155]

From Cardenas, the party subsequently traveled by private railway car to Havana, where they were met by a large and enthusiastic crowd. They were now the esteemed guests of Governor General Dulce, who, on the evening of 14 June, hosted a private dinner for Wood, Breckinridge, and Charles J. Helm, the former Confederate agent in Havana. During the course of the evening, the governor general's three Confederate guests were all offered asylum in Cuba. Wood, who at this juncture, naturally assumed that he would face prosecution for his role in the war, was extremely grateful for such hospitality; however, he had chosen another place of exile for himself and his family. Like so many of the defeated Loyalists following America's first civil war during the American Revolution, he would go North, seeking refuge in British North America.[156]

Chapter 6

Exile in Halifax, Nova Scotia, 1865–1904

Wood had decided that his best course of action would be to arrange for his family to meet him in Montreal, Canada East. Consequently, he began to seek passage to British North America. Although he was, at first, reluctant to sail on one of the many Confederate steam blockade runners then in Cuba, assuming that they would still be subject to capture by the North, he finally relented and tentatively arranged to ship with former CSN commander John Newland Maffitt on the *Owl*. However, legal problems with Maffitt's vessel soon prompted Wood to approach an old friend, George E. Shyrock, late of the warship CSS *Stonewall*, who had been charged with the delivery of the blockade runner *Lark* to England, by way of Halifax, Nova Scotia. In choosing Shyrock's vessel, the last steam blockade runner to clear a Confederate port, Wood was mindful of her record: "The *Lark* is not fast, but she has been a lucky ship, has never been chased." Fortunately for Wood, the ship's luck persisted. Leaving Cuba on 23 June, she arrived in Halifax on 30 June. The trip was largely uneventful; however, the vessel did almost run aground twice as she penetrated the thick fog in Halifax harbor.[157]

After spending several days with Shyrock on board the *Lark* at Halifax, Wood took passage on the steamer *Queen Victoria*, bound for Quebec City. He arrived in the historic city on the evening of 9 July and spent the following day visiting the sights, including the Plains of Abraham, the scene, in 1759, of one of Britain's greatest military victories. On 11 July, Wood boarded a steamer for Montreal, where he booked into the Donegana Hotel, which he deemed "a good house." Four days later, he had a joyful reunion with his wife, Lola, and his two children, five-year-old Zachary and the baby Lola, who had been born in Richmond less than a month before Lee's surrender.[158] Once he was reunited with his family, Wood's next concern was to choose a place of exile in British North America. Although many prominent Confederate expatriates were then settling in Canada East (present-day Quebec) and West (now Ontario), Wood decided to take his family to the city of Halifax, located in the maritime province of Nova Scotia. The reasons for his decision are not difficult to surmise.

Firstly, as the commander of the *Tallahassee* in 1864, Wood had already established connections with Halifax's Confederate agent, Benjamin Wier, as well as with Dr. W.J. Almon and other prominent members of the city's large pro-Confederate faction. In fact, during his brief stay in Halifax in early July 1865, Wood had met with Wier, receiving not only the remaining money in the *Tallahassee's* account, but also, in all likelihood, an invitation to make Halifax his new home.[159] The support of Wier and other key members of the Halifax elite offered Wood not only a welcoming political and social environment, but also the promise of business opportunities.

Secondly, because Halifax was a major port and a British naval station, Wood no doubt realized that he could likely maintain his connection with the sea by pursuing a maritime career in the city. Thirdly, Nova Scotia was located in a largely non-industrial region that, like the South, was somewhat marginalized in terms of political and economic power. As a staunchly British colony, the province was also distrustful of its powerful Yankee neighbors to the South. However, having been settled primarily by New England planters, and then by Loyalists, Nova Scotia had strong economic links with America and shared with it a common language and heritage. The province even had a significant population of blacks. Finally, a short-lived but sizable colony of Confederates, including many former members of the CSN, was starting to take shape in Nova Scotia, particularly in Halifax, thus providing Wood and other Southern expatriates with an important network of mutual support.[160]

The Wood family arrived in Halifax in the late summer of 1865. During the next few months, they and other Southern refugees began to settle into their new lives in the Nova Scotian capital. Meanwhile, events were unfolding in the northeastern United States that would soon offer Wood and other Confederate veterans in Nova Scotia what appeared to be an unexpected opportunity to once again fight their Yankee foes, this time serving under the Union Jack.

Following the Civil War, relations between the United States and Britain were severely strained. The victorious Northern states were in a bellicose mood and were determined to make Britain pay for the role it had played in the war, particularly with regard to the construction of the notorious CSN commerce raiders that had preyed so successfully upon Union shipping. Among those who sought to take advantage of American post-war hostility toward the United Kingdom were the Fenians, militant Irish nationalists bent on undermining British interests in the hope of promoting Irish independence. One of their primary targets was Britain's colonies in North America. In March 1866, Nova's Scotia's neighboring province, New Brunswick, was threatened by the revolutionary organization the Fenian Brotherhood, which had purchased a former Confederate schooner, the *Ocean Spray*, and had assembled a sizable invasion force, composed mostly of Union army veterans, in Eastport, Calais, and other border communities in Maine. A major confrontation seemed imminent, and local militias and home-guard forces in British North America were hurriedly mobilized to defend against the Fenian invaders.[161]

The Halifax-area Confederate community quickly responded to the Yankee threat to their new home. On 19 March, Wood contacted Benjamin Wier and asked him to forward a hastily prepared petition to the lieutenant governor of Nova Scotia, Sir Fenwick Williams. Dated 17 March, St. Patrick's Day, the day that the Fenian attack was expected to begin, the document read as follows: "Having adopted Nova Scotia as our homes, we undersigned, late citizens of the Confederate States do hereby tender our services in the defense of the province; in the present emergency." The petition was signed by Wood and twelve other Confederates, including such CSN veterans in Halifax and Dartmouth as Richard Fielder Armstrong, Francis Lyell Hoge, Charles Schroeder, John Wilkinson, and George T. Sinclair.[162]

As it turned out, Nova Scotia did not find it necessary to call upon the Confederate exiles in its midst. Following a few minor incidents, the Fenians' invasion plans were thwarted by the intervention of U.S. General George Meade, the Union victor at Gettysburg, who seized the Fenians' main arms shipment, and by the arrival of several British gunboats in Pasmaquoddy Bay, where the Irish nationalists had hoped to strike a blow for Ireland by seizing the island of Campobello. Although the Halifax Confederate's petition did not, after all, result in a final, belated clash between remnants of the Confederate States Navy and the detested Yankee enemy, it did testify to the fact that many of the Southern refugees in Nova Scotia were not yet ready to make peace with those who had conquered the Confederacy. This was especially true of Wood, who appears to have organized the petition. Increasingly, his allegiance was now to his new home.

Less than a year after the Fenian scare, on February 1867, Wood and some of the other Confederate signatories of the 1866 petition had

Wood's business partner, CSN veteran John Wilkinson (*History of the Confederate Navy*).

occasion to once again act as a community and collectively sign a document, this time a letter of condolence to Dr. W.J. Almon, whose son Bruce, a CSA veteran, died unexpectedly at Halifax.[163] It was especially important for Wood to express his sympathy to Almon. Not only had Jefferson Davis previously thanked the Halifax physician for his many services to the Confederacy, but Almon, who had provided assistance to Wood during the *Tallahassee's* controversial visit to Halifax in 1864, had subsequently become a good friend, and had, in fact, by this time, helped Wood establish himself in business in Halifax.[164]

Wood's transformation from Rebel warrior to businessman began shortly after his arrival in Nova Scotia. His first commercial venture was a wholesale merchant house. In addition to assistance from Almon, he received support from Wier and from the Wood family in Maryland, with whom he had finally reconciled. Initially, Wood was in partnership with another Confederate naval hero, John Wilkinson. Fittingly, their firm, Wilkinson, Wood and Company, specialized in "Southern produce." It also represented several British and American firms, including the Liverpool-based merchant house co-owned by James Dunwoody Bulloch, the Confederacy's former naval agent in Britain. For a time, Wilkinson and Wood were joined by a third CSN veteran, Charles Schroeder, who, as an engineer, had served with Wood on the CSS *Virginia*. Following Wilkinson's return to the United States in the early 1870s, the merchant house was renamed Wood and Company. Located in a warehouse overlooking Halifax harbor, the firm often defiantly flew the Confederate star and bars, much to the chagrin, no doubt, of the local American consul.[165]

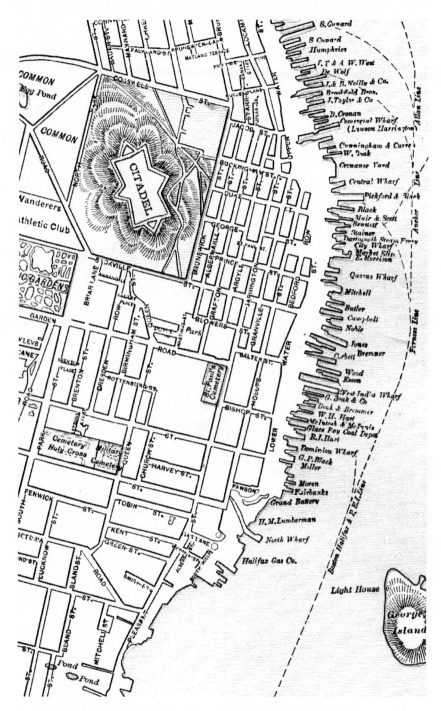

A portion of the Halifax waterfront, c. 1891, showing Wood's wharf near the bottom of Salter Saint (*Cram's Unrivaled Family Atlas of the World*).

Wood's commercial interests were not confined to his activities as a wholesale merchant. Eventually he was engaged in real-estate speculation and several other businesses, including the Block House Coal Mining Company, the Eastern Steamship Company, the Atlantic Marine Insurance Association, and the Boston Marine Insurance Company. A member of the Chamber of Commerce, he was also an agent for the Cromwell Line. As well, starting in 1874, he served on the Halifax Pilot Commission.[166]

However, not all Wood's enterprises were successful. His involvement with the Cromwell Line, which was plagued by the loss of a number of vessels, eventually became a liability, even though he was able to rush to the scene of one major disaster, involving the ship *Cortes*, which ran aground on Thrum Cap Shoal outside Halifax harbor, and save the vessel's passengers and cargo.[167] Financial reversals in other areas eventually followed, resulting in the failure, in the late 1880s, of his wholesale firm and other business ventures. As a consequence, Wood was forced to sell most of his property, leaving him with two main sources of income: his position with the Halifax Pilot Commission and his role as the Halifax agent for the Boston Marine Insurance Company.[168]

In his capacity as secretary of the Halifax Pilot Commission, Wood emerged as one of the Nova Scotian capital's leading promoters. A prolific writer of letters to the editors of local newspapers, he supported a variety of development schemes for Halifax, all of which were intended to transform the sleepy Bluenose port into a more progressive and dynamic transatlantic shipping center. Among the causes that he championed were the completion of the Intercolonial Railway linking the British North American colonies, the construction of a rail connection between Halifax and New York, the building of a modern dry-dock facility, and the reduction of port charges to attract larger transatlantic vessels. He also sought to promote Halifax as a tourist destination and pushed for the establishment of a training ship designed to teach maritime skills to underprivileged children.[169]

As an agent for the Boston Marine Insurance Association, Wood was further involved in the maritime life of his adopted home. However, his duties in the insurance field could sometimes be grim. In 1896, he was one of the first people to board the U.S. barkentine *Herbert Fuller*, which arrived in Halifax on 21 July, towing a jolly boat that held the bodies of the vessel's captain, his wife, and the second mate, all of whom had been butchered by an ax-wielding crew member. The carnage that Wood likely witnessed that day must have reminded him of some of his more gruesome experiences as a naval raider.[170]

Despite the vicissitudes of his mercantile career, Wood was firmly ensconced as a prominent member of Halifax polite society. Appropriately, given his naval background, during his early years in the city he became an active yachtsman, joining the Royal Halifax Yacht Club (RHYC), probably in 1867, during his friend Wier's tenure as the club's commodore. Not surprisingly, Wood proved to be a very competitive sailor. In 1872, his yacht *Whisper*, which he had acquired in 1870, won the prestigious Prince of Wales Cup. After serving as the RHYC's vice-commodore from 1871 to 1873, Wood became commodore in 1874, for a one-year term.[171] A few years later, he further solidified his social position by building a stately home on fashionable Morris Street, not far from St. Luke's, the Anglican church where he and his growing family (seven children would be born in Halifax between 1866 and 1876) worshipped.[172] A devout churchman, Wood became a prominent and active member of the Anglican community in Halifax.[173]

The standing of the Wood family in the garrison city of Halifax was also enhanced by the careers of two of Wood's sons, who chose to follow in their father's footsteps. Zachary, Wood's eldest boy, graduated from the Royal Military College (RMC) in Kingston, Ontario, in 1882. Ironically, for the son of a Rebel, in 1885 he served with the Winnipeg Battalion of the 90th Infantry Regiment in the suppression of the Northwest Rebellion, a sectional uprising against Canada's central government. Following the Rebellion, Zachary joined the North-West Mounted Police and would go on to a distinguished career in the Mounties, eventually rising to the position of assistant commissioner.[174] Another son, Charles, Wood's youngest, also attended RMC. Upon graduation in 1896, he joined the British Army and saw service in India. Following the outbreak of the Boer War in October 1899, he was dispatched to South Africa. Much to Wood's dismay, on 10 November 1899, Charles, then serving as a lieutenant with the Loyal North Lancashire Regiment, was fatally wounded in action near Belmont, becoming the first Canadian to fall in the conflict.[175] Several weeks later, the British monarch herself, Queen Victoria, conveyed her sympathy and then requested a picture of Charles, which Wood supplied, no doubt with considerable pride. Among the many other people who expressed their condolences to Wood was Robert E. Lee, Jr., who had met Charles during a visit to Halifax three years earlier.[176]

Wood and his family also received more public expressions of sympathy. The children of Morris Street School honored Charles Wood by planting a tree in Halifax's Public Gardens and marking it with a commemorative plaque.[177] Later, the community of Taylorville in Halifax County was renamed Chaswood.[178] Finally, Charles would eventually be honored on the South African soldier's monument erected on the grounds of Province House in Halifax. The cornerstone of the monument was laid in October 1901 by the Duke (who would later reign as George V) and Duchess of York and Cornwall, then on a royal tour.

Although Wood had become a distinguished member of the Halifax social and mercantile elite, he enjoyed a particularly wide circle of friends that cut across class lines. Perhaps one of his most unlikely friendships was with a USN veteran, a black sailor named William Hall, who resided at Horton Bluff in Nova Scotia's Kings County. Following his service in the USN, Hall had joined the British navy, becoming, in 1857, the first black and first Canadian sailor to win the coveted Victoria Cross (VC), Britain's greatest military honor. At some point in the 1880s or 1890s, Wood learned about Hall, who was then retired and, despite an impressive military record, living in near poverty. Once Wood realized that he and Hall had served together on the USS *Ohio* during the Mexican War, he visited his old shipmate, and the two naval veterans, one a descendant of a slave family from Maryland and the other an unreconstructed Confederate from the same state, became unlikely friends. Concerned about Hall's living conditions, Wood endeavoured to help the VC winner obtain a Mexican War pension — without success.[179]

Although Wood came to be a staunch Bluenose, and stubbornly lived out his life in permanent exile in Nova Scotia, ignoring various Federal amnesty proclamations, he did not entirely turn his back on America. In fact, he visited his native country on several occasions.[180] One of his most memorable trips occurred in May 1890, when, at the behest of the Lee family, he returned to Richmond for the unveiling of the city's imposing Robert E. Lee monument. This event was one of the great post-war gatherings of the Confederacy. On 29 May, the day of the unveiling, Wood participated in a grand procession to Monument Avenue, riding at the front of the parade in the last of eight carriages reserved for Confederate dignitaries.[181] In March 1892, he returned to Virginia, this time traveling to Norfolk to celebrate the thirtieth anniversary of the duel between the *Virginia* and the *Monitor*. Here Wood met one of his former foes, the *Monitor's* commander, John L. Worden, now an admiral in the USN. One newspaper account of the event made note of Wood's impressive bearing: "time has dealt kindly with him, and through [sic] his locks are silvered, his tall and strong body is erect; his step elastic." During his visit to Norfolk, Wood was also reunited with Benjamin P. Loyall, who had served as second-in-command in the capture of the USS *Underwriter*.[182]

Wood's efforts to maintain his connection with the glory days of what he called "The Great Cause" were not confined to his attendance at a number of important Southern reunions.[183] Like so many of the war's participants, he also contributed, although somewhat belatedly, to the deluge of veterans' reminiscences and other war-related literature that appeared following the Civil War. (Some of the other Confederates who lived, at least for a time, in exile in Nova Scotia — including John Wilkinson, Randolph Stevenson, Frank L. Hoge, and Richard Fielder Armstrong — also wrote about their wartime experiences or other aspects of the war.)

Much of this post-war writing appeared in series that sought to combine both Union and Confederate perspectives of the war's events. The most notable of these appeared in *The Philadelphia Weekly Times*, starting in 1877, and in *The Century Illustrated Monthly Magazine*, beginning in 1884. Selected contributions to both series were subsequently published in book form. The *Century* collection, the massive, four-volume *Battles and Leaders of the Civil War* (1887–1888), remains one of the most-utilized sources on the war. In addition to periodicals that strove to offer a balanced picture of the war, there were more partisan publications. The three most important pro-Confederate journals were the *Southern Historical Society Papers* (1876–1959), *Southern Bivouac* (1882–1886), and *Confederate Veteran* (1893–1932). All three publications played a significant role in shaping a Southern post-war consciousness and in promulgating and sustaining the mythology of the Lost Cause.[184]

Although Wood had been contacted in 1873 by William Preston Johnston of the Southern Historical Society and urged to write his war memoirs in order to "add a valuable chapter to the History of the War," he did not feel compelled to write about the Civil War until 1880, when, at the request of Jefferson Davis, who was then at work on *The Rise and Fall of the Confederate Government* (1881), Wood prepared an eight-page summary history of the Confederate navy.[185] He also apparently provided some assistance to J. Thomas Scharf, who, as a midshipman, had served under him in the capture of the USS *Underwriter*.[186] Scharf's massive *History of the Confederate States Navy from Its Organization to the Surrender of its Last Vessel* finally appeared in 1887.

Wood did not start to write about his own war experiences until the latter part of the 1880s, about the same time that he was experiencing serious setbacks in his business career. His first published article was "The First Fight of Iron-Clads," a history of the CSS *Virginia*, which he contributed in March 1885 to the *Century Illustrated Monthly Magazine's* prestigious series of "war papers." Two years later, the piece was reprinted in the first volume of *Battles and Leaders of the Civil War*. (Just as he began to reflect on the war, Wood was invited to join another leading institution of the Halifax elite, the Nova Scotia Historical Society.)[187] Wood's next Civil War memoir, "Running the Blockade at Halifax," an account of the *Tallahassee's* cruise, appeared in August 1889 in the *Carnival Echo*, a special issue of a Halifax paper. In November 1893, he published "Escape of the Confederate Secretary of War," a powerful memoir recounting his escape to Cuba at the war's end (this article was later collected in the anthology *Famous Adventures and Prison Escapes of the Civil War*, issued in 1904).

Wood was proving himself to be an accomplished writer. Not surprisingly, his war memoirs contributed significantly to his celebrity in Halifax. In 1896, his exploits as commander of the *Tallahassee* were fictionalized in a juvenile novel by the Halifax writer James MacDonald Oxley. In Oxley's popular novel about Confederate blockade running, *Baffling the Blockade*, the *Tallahassee's* nighttime escape from Halifax was attributed to another vessel, the fictional *Greyhound*.[188] It is very likely that Wood and Oxley, a lawyer who specialized in maritime law and later worked for a major insurance company, were at least acquaintances. (Wood was definitely acquainted with the Halifax writer Alice Jones, who presented him with an inscribed copy of her novel about Confederate blockade runners, *The Night-hawk: A Romance of the 60's*, which was published in 1901 under the pseudonym Alix John.)[189]

In 1897 Wood was asked to address the Philomathic Society of Dalhousie College. His well-attended lecture, on the evening of 15 January, was devoted to the topic of Lee and his generals, and drew on Wood's personal experiences. According to the *Dalhousie Gazette*, Wood's talk was a resounding success: "Seldom has a lecturer at Dalhousie received such breathless attention, and such enthusiastic and long-continued applause, as was accorded the old hero of the South."[190]

Just over a year later, the Philomathic Society induced Wood to "sacrifice his modesty" and return for a second lecture, this time devoted to the *Tallahassee*, a subject which was becoming increasingly dear to the hearts of Haligonians.[191] Entitled "A Cruise on a Blockade Runner," this text represented his second attempt at narrating the vessel's story. The first part of this lecture was printed in two Halifax newspapers on 14 and 15 February 1898.[192] A week later, Wood was in the local press again, this time with a brief article speculating on the cause of the sinking of the battleship USS *Maine* in Havana harbor.[193] Not long after, he published "The *Tallahassee's* Dash into New York Waters" in *Century* magazine. This was Wood's third account of the cruise of the Confederate warship and proved to be his final Civil War memoir.

Regrettably, Wood stopped writing about the war before he could describe his adventures as one of the Confederacy's most daring commandos. Given his modesty, it is likely that he made a conscious decision to leave the depiction of this aspect of his Confederate service to those who had served under him. In any event, Wood's literary efforts did not cease in 1898. In 1899, he contributed a brief survey of Halifax's history and it advantages as a port, "Halifax, the Open Door of Canada," to *The Canadian Magazine*, one of Canada's leading periodicals. The following year, he published another compelling military memoir, this time devoted to an incident from his years as a midshipman in the U.S. Navy. Entitled "The Capture of a Slaver," the piece appeared in *Atlantic Monthly* (October 1900) and was then reprinted in the Halifax *Evening Mail*. As well, in 1902 or thereabouts, Wood wrote an account of the distinguished naval career of his friend William Hall, the black Nova Scotian who had served with him on the USS *Ohio*. (This article remained unpublished until November 1904, when one of Wood's British military friends, Major B.R. Ward of the Royal Engineers, arranged for it to appear in the *Halifax Herald*.)

Halifax's hero, the unreconstructed rebel, c. 1895 (*Nova Scotia Archives and Records Management N-9221*).

Probably sometime in 1903, Wood embarked on his most ambitious literary project: a full-fledged autobiography.[194] Regrettably, before he could complete work on his reminiscences, Wood fell ill with a severe bout of influenza. In the spring of 1904, he made a partial recovery and resumed work at his office.[195] During this time, he authenticated a chart depicting the CSS *Tallahassee*'s precise route out of Halifax harbor through the Eastern Passage in 1864.[196] He then spent a few weeks recuperating at Wolfville, in Nova Scotia's Annapolis Valley. However, upon his return to Halifax in late June, he became ill again, and after three weeks of confinement, the old Rebel died at home, on the morning of 19 July, unreconstructed to the end.[197] (Among the effects found in his office after his death was a tantalizing thirty-five-page manuscript covering the first twenty years of his eventful life.)[198]

Another prominent Confederate expatriate in Halifax, Richard Fielder Armstrong, best known for his service as a lieutenant on the *Alabama*, had predeceased Wood by just a few months.[199] Armstrong's passing had prompted several small notices in the local papers. Wood's death was an entirely different matter. The city had long before claimed the *Tallahassee*'s commander as one of its great heroes and leading citizens. Accordingly, his death was a major news story and the cause of much lamentation in his adopted home. *The Morning Chronicle* expressed the sorrow felt by many Haligonians: "Captain Wood was an excellent representative of the type of the Southern gentleman, with a wide culture and excellent scientific attainments. His familiar form will be missed from amongst us, but his name will be held in high esteem and loving memory not only for his daring exploits, for his interest time and again manifested in this city's welfare both in social and mercantile life, but for his contribution to the British Empire."[200] *The Evening Mail* echoed these sentiments: "The announcement of the death of Captain John Taylor Wood, which took place at his residence shortly after eight this morning will be received with universal sorrow and regret. None in Halifax were more esteemed than he, and few had so wide a circle of friends."[201]

On Thursday, 21 July, Wood's remains were taken from his home on Morris Street to St. Luke's Cathedral. Following the funeral service, his body was conveyed to Camp Hill Cemetery for internment.[202] At the time of his death, Wood had been serving as the Halifax Pilot Commission's secretary-treasurer. As a result, six of the city's pilots served as his pall-bearers. Furthermore, as his hearse made its way to Camp Hill, it was preceded by a larger group of pilots. At Camp Hill, Wood was buried in the family plot. Nearby were the graves of two Wood children, May (1875–1898) and Robert Crooke (1866–1884). In 1909, Lola would join her husband and children. Wood's surviving sons would later erect a stone monument to their parents. The gravestone made no mention of John Taylor Wood's distinguished military service. In addition to John Taylor and Lola Wood's names and dates, it bore only a simple inscription: "They Rest From Their Labours."[203]

Chapter 7

A Rebel's Legacy

Following his death, Wood remained a hero to the people of Halifax, who took considerable pride in the fact that such a distinguished Confederate expatriate had chosen to live out his life in their midst. Haligonians were especially proud of their city's connection with the CSS *Tallahassee*. Accordingly, the cruiser's voyage through the Eastern Passage in 1864 — a very minor episode in Wood's eventful naval career — continued to loom large in Halifax's mythology. In fact, in the 1920s and 1930s, when a strong regional identity was taking shape in Nova Scotia and the province was in search of its own distinctive heroes, the story of Wood and the *Tallahassee* was woven into the fabric of a larger regional mythology.

For many decades, Wood's account of the *Tallahassee's* escape from Halifax was even reprinted in provincial school readers in Nova Scotia.[204] Furthermore, numerous Nova Scotian authors (see the annotated bibliography) celebrated Wood's accomplishments, particularly his role as the *Tallahassee's* commander. One of the most prominent of these writers was Arthur Hunt Chute, who, as a child, had heard the story of the *Tallahassee* directly from Wood himself.[205] For Chute and many others, Wood ranked as one of the great Bluenose skippers, belonging as much to Nova Scotia as to the Confederacy. The efforts to claim Wood as a Nova Scotian hero reached a culmination in 1945, with the publication of Andrew Merkel's book-length narrative poem *Tallahassee: A Ballad of Nova Scotia in the Sixties*, which explored Nova Scotia's connection with the Confederacy during the Civil War.[206]

Although Wood and the *Tallahassee* no longer occupy such a central place in Halifax's identity, during the past fifty years or so the city where he lived for more than half his life has certainly not forgotten him. In 1955, the elementary school in Eastern Passage, the community that overlooks the narrow channel that the *Tallahassee* negotiated in 1864, was named after Wood's cruiser.[207] Furthermore, Wood and his exploits have figured in a variety of

Nova Scotian publications, including *Tallahassee Skipper*, a long, rambling biography by local historian Arthur Thurston. As well, in the 1980s, the province of Nova Scotia even utilized the story of Wood and the *Tallahassee* in a tourism campaign aimed at Civil War enthusiasts.[208] While Wood remains little-known elsewhere in Canada — except in Royal Canadian Mounted Police (RCMP) circles, where he has received some recognition as the progenitor of one of the force's major dynas-

ties (Wood's grandson, Stuart Taylor Wood, served as the commissioner of the RCMP) — it is clear that he has become a permanent part of Nova Scotia's heritage. This is confirmed, perhaps, by the fact that his account of the *Tallahassee's* departure from Halifax has, during the past decade or so, been challenged by a few Halifax-based researchers, one of whom has even suggested that the story is a complete fabrication.[209] Such revisionist efforts testify to the fact that the *Tallahassee* and her commander have left their mark on Nova Scotia.

Although Wood has long been recognized in his adopted home, his reputation in the United States since his death in 1904 has not always been so prominent. Even though he was the subject of a thesis at Southern Methodist University in 1935 and also figured prominently in A.J. Hanna's book on the flight of the Confederate cabinet, *Flight into Oblivion* (1938), awareness of Wood's accomplishments remained rather limited and

Wood's grave in Camp Hill Cemetery, Halifax, Nova Scotia [see note no. 203] (*John Bell photo*).

sporadic until 1979, when Royce Gordon Shingleton's excellent biography, *John Taylor Wood: Sea Ghost of the Confederacy*, was published by the University of Georgia.[210] Since the appearance of Shingleton's book, interest in and recognition of the role of the Confederate States Navy in the Civil War has increased markedly. As this attention has increased, so has Wood's stature.

Despite the fact that the historical record does not provide a complete picture of Wood's dual role as a combatant and as a key advisor on Confederate naval policy, there is more than ample evidence of his exceptional competence and daring. He was, as Jefferson Davis put it, "an officer of extraordinary ability and enterprise."[211] Today his reputation as a leading Confederate naval hero is secure. For instance, in his recent — and authoritative — study *A History of the Confederate Navy* (1996), the Italian historian Raimond Luraghi devotes half a chapter to Wood, whom he characterizes as one of the great Confederate naval commanders, part of "an elite rarely found in naval history."[212]

In both his native land and his adopted country, Wood's ultimate legacy is, perhaps, one of defiant heroism. Compelled by honor and duty to serve the Confederacy, he committed himself fully to the Confederate cause, fighting with great distinction and refusing at the war's end to surrender to the South's conquerors. Instead, like the American Loyalists almost a century before, he risked his life to reach a place of exile where he could escape retribution and remain true to the British-American ideals and heritage that had shaped his life. Under the Union Jack, his third flag, in the seaside province of Nova Scotia, far removed from the seats of power and industrial might, he discovered a kindred people. While most Confederate expatriates in Canada eventually returned to the new, reconstructed America, Wood came to realize that he was already home, living in a place where his service in the Lost Cause would be respected, if not admired. He was, in a sense, a late Loyalist.

Towards the end of his life, Wood described his fellow Nova Scotians this way: "Sturdy men from England, Scotland and Ireland, with a little seasoning of American loyalists, make up a strain not excelled."[213] He, too, obviously belonged to such a strain. Even if one agrees with Ulysses S. Grant's blunt assertion that the Confederate cause was "one of the worst for which a people ever fought," one must nonetheless admire the unfaltering faith and courage displayed time and time again by Wood in his service to the Confederacy.[214] In a tragic, internecine war that he had tried to avoid, Wood achieved greatness. By remaining unreconstructed to the end, he defiantly and stubbornly adhered to the ideals that had led him to that greatness.

PART TWO

The Civil War Memoirs of a Confederate Exile: Writings of John Taylor Wood

A Note on the Text

The three memoirs that comprise Part Two were chosen from the various Civil War–related texts that were written by John Taylor Wood during his years in Halifax (see Appendix 4). Although all of the selected articles originally appeared in *The Century Illustrated Monthly Magazine*, two of them were later reprinted, with some revisions, by Century Co. in two compilations of Civil War narratives. The precise sources for the versions of these texts that appear in *Confederate Seadog* are identified in the headnotes that precede the three memoirs. The original spelling and punctuation in all three texts have been retained, although misspellings and typographical errors have been corrected.

Chapter 8

The First Fight of
Iron-Clads

"The First Fight of Iron-Clads," Wood's first published memoir devoted to his Civil War experiences, initially appeared in The Century Illustrated Monthly Magazine *(March 1885). A slightly abridged and revised version of the piece was later reprinted in the first book of the four-volume collection* Battles and Leaders of the Civil War *(1887-1888), edited by Robert U. Johnson and Clarence C. Buel. Significant portions of the memoir also appeared much later in* Combat: The Civil War *(1967), edited by Don Congdon.*

The version that follows is based mostly on the slightly revised and corrected text that appeared in Battles and Leaders of the Civil War; *however, the last two paragraphs of the original* Century *article, which were deleted by Johnson and Buel, have been restored. It should also be noted that the footnotes which originally accompanied the piece have not been included, as they were mostly added by the editors at* Century *and contribute little of importance to Wood's narrative.*

In the article, Wood details his service in 1862 as a lieutenant on the first Confederate ironclad, CSS Virginia *(formerly USS* Merrimack). *In addition to providing a first-hand account of the vessel's destruction of the USS* Cumberland *and the USS* Congress *on 8 March and of her historic battle with the USS* Monitor *on the following day, Wood describes the second encounter between the crew of the* Virginia *and the Union ironclad in May 1862 at Drewery's Bluff, Virginia.*

The piece sheds some light as well on the career of the Virginia's *second commander, Captain (later Commodore) Josiah Tattnall,*

who, from 1866 to 1870, joined Wood and other prominent Confederate exiles in Halifax. Also mentioned in the narrative is Sir James
Hope, who would later serve as the commander of the British naval
squadron at Halifax during Wood's visit to the port as the commander of the Confederate raider CSS Tallahassee (see Wood's second
memoir). Wood also refers to another British commander, William
Hewett, who would become a famous blockade-runner and one of
Wood's wartime friends.

The illustrations accompanying Wood's memoir are reprinted
from the March 1885 issue of The Century Illustrated Monthly
Magazine.

Although Wood settled in Halifax in 1865, he did return to the
United States on several occasions, including a trip to Norfolk in
March 1892 to commemorate the thirtieth anniversary of the first
battle between ironclad vessels. During this visit he met with old
comrades and with his former adversary, the Monitor's commander,
John L. Worden.

The illustrations accompanying Wood's memoir are reprinted
from the March 1885 issue of The Century Illustrated Monthly
Magazine.

THE FIRST FIGHT OF IRON-CLADS

The engagement in Hampton Roads on the 8th of March, 1862,
between the Confederate iron-clad *Virginia*, or the *Merrimac* (as she is
known at the North), and the United States wooden fleet, and that on the
9th between the *Virginia* and the *Monitor*, was, in its results, in some
respects the most momentous naval conflict ever witnessed.[215] No battle
was ever more widely discussed or produced a greater sensation. It revolutionized the navies of the world. Line-of-battle ships, those huge, over-
grown craft, carrying from eighty to one hundred and twenty guns and
from five hundred to twelve hundred men, which from the destruction of
the Spanish Armada to our time, had done most of the fighting, deciding
the fates of empires, were at once universally condemned as out of date.
Rams and iron-clads were in future to decide all naval warfare. In this battle old things passed away, and the experience of a thousand years of battle and breeze was forgotten. The naval supremacy of England vanished
in the smoke of this fight, it is true, only to reappear some years later more
commanding than ever. The effect of the news was best described by the
London *Times*, which said: "Whereas we had available for immediate pur-
poses one hundred and forty-nine first-class war-ships, we have now two,
these two being the *Warrior* and her sister *Ironside*. There is not now a ship

"The United States frigate 'Merrimac' before and after conversion into an Iron-Clad" (*The Century Illustrated Monthly Magazine*, March 1885).

in the English navy apart from these two that it would not be madness to trust to an engagement with that little *Monitor*." The Admiralty at once proceeded to reconstruct the navy, cutting down a number of their largest ships and converting them into turret or broadside iron-clads. The same results were produced in France, which had but one sea-going iron-clad, *La Gloire*, and this one, like the *Warrior*, was only protected amidships. The Emperor Napoleon promptly appointed a commission to devise plans for rebuilding his navy. And so with all the maritime powers. In this race the United States took the lead, and at the close of the war led all the others in the numbers and efficiency of its iron-clad fleet. It is true that all the great powers had already experimented with vessels partly armored, but very few were convinced of their utility, and none had been tried by the test of battle, if we except a few floating batteries, thinly clad, used in the Crimean War.

In the spring of 1861 Norfolk and its large naval establishment had been hurriedly abandoned by the Federals, why no one could tell. It is about twelve miles from Fort Monroe, which was then held by a large force of regulars. A few companies of these, with a single frigate, could have occupied and commanded the town and navy yard and kept the channel

"Burning of the frigate 'Merrimac' and the Norfolk Navy-yard" (*The Century Illustrated Monthly Magazine*, March 1885).

open. However, a year later, it was as quickly evacuated by the Confederates, and almost with as little reason. But of this I will speak later.

The yard was abandoned to a few volunteers, after it was partly destroyed, and a large number of ships were burnt. Among the spoils were upward of twelve hundred heavy guns, which were scattered among Confederate fortifications from the Potomac to the Mississippi. Among the ships burnt and sunk was the frigate *Merrimac* of 3500 tons and 40 guns, afterward rechristened the *Virginia*, and so I will call her. During the summer of 1861 Lieutenant John M. Brooke, an accomplished officer of the old navy, who with many others had resigned, proposed to Secretary Mallory to raise and rebuild this ship as an iron-clad. His plans were approved, and

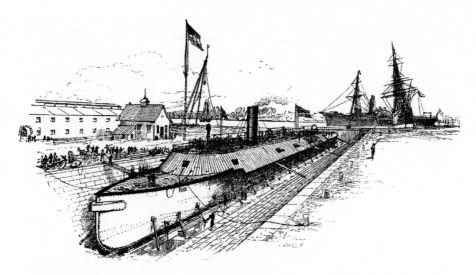

"Remodeling the 'Merrimac' at the Norfolk Navy-yard" (*The Century Illustrated Monthly Magazine*, March 1885).

orders were given to carry them out. She was raised and cut down to the old berth-deck. Both ends for seventy feet were covered over, and when the ship was in fighting trim were just awash. On the midship section, 170 feet in length, was built at an angle of 45 degrees a roof of pitch-pine and oak 24 inches thick, extending from the water-line to a height over the gun-deck of 7 feet. Both ends of the shield were rounded so that the pivot-guns could be used as bow and stern chasers or quartering. Over the gun-deck was a light grating, making a promenade about twenty feet wide. The wood backing was covered with iron plates, rolled at the Tredegar works, two inches thick and eight wide. The first tier was put on horizontally, the second up and down, — in all to the thickness of four inches, bolted through the wood-work and clinched. The prow was of cast-iron, projecting four feet, and badly secured, as events proved. The rudder and propeller were entirely unprotected. The pilot-house was forward of the smoke-stack, and covered with the same thickness of iron as the sides. The motive power was the same that had always been in the ship. Both of the engines and boilers had been condemned on her return from her last cruise, and were radically defective. Of course, the fire and sinking had not improved them. We could not depend upon them for six hours at a time. A more ill-contrived or unreliable pair of engines could only have been found in some vessels of the United States navy.

Lieutenant Catesby ap R. Jones was ordered to superintend the armament, and no more thoroughly competent officer could have been selected.

To his experience and skill as her ordnance and executive officer was due the character of her battery, which proved so efficient. It consisted of 2 7-inch rifles, heavily reënforced around the breech with 3-inch steel bands, shrunk on. These were the first heavy guns so made, and were the bow and stern pivots. There were also 2 6-inch rifles of the same make, and 6 9-inch smooth-bore broadside — 10 guns in all.

During the summer and fall of 1861 I had been stationed at the batteries on the Potomac at Evansport and Aquia Creek, blockading the river as far as possible. In January, 1862, I was ordered to the *Virginia* as one of the lieutenants, reporting to Commodore French Forrest, who

"Lieutenant Catesby ap R. Jones (from a photograph by Courret Hermanos, Lima) (*The Century Illustrated Monthly Magazine*, March 1885).

then commanded the navy yard at Norfolk. Commodore Franklin Buchanan was appointed to the command, — an energetic and high-toned officer, who combined with daring courage great professional ability, standing deservedly at the head of his profession. In 1845 he had been selected by Mr. Bancroft, Secretary of the Navy, to locate and organize the Naval Academy, and he launched that institution upon its successful career. Under him were as capable a set of officers as ever were brought together in one ship. But of man-of-war's men or sailors we had scarcely any. The South was almost without a maritime population. In the old service the majority of officers were from the South, and all the seamen from the North.

Every one had flocked to the army, and to it we had to look for a crew. Some few seamen were found in Norfolk, who had escaped from the gunboat flotilla in the waters of North Carolina, on their occupation by Admiral Goldsborough and General Burnside. In hopes of securing some men from the army, I was sent to the headquarters of General Magruder at Yorktown, who was known to have under his command two battalions from New Orleans, among whom might be found a number of seamen. The general, though pressed for want of men, holding a long line with scarcely a brigade, gave me every facility to secure volunteers. With one of his staff I visited every camp, and the commanding officers were ordered to parade their men, and I explained to them what I wanted. About 200 volunteered, and of this number I selected 80 who had some experience as seamen or gunners. Other commands at Richmond and Petersburg were visited, and so our crew of three hundred was made up. They proved themselves to be as gallant and trusty a body of men as any one would wish to command, not only in battle, but in reverse and retreat.

Notwithstanding every exertion to hasten the fitting out of the ship, the work during the winter progressed but slowly, owing to delay in sending the iron sheathing from Richmond. At this time the only establishment in the South capable of rolling iron plates was the Tredegar foundry. Its resources were limited, and demand for all kinds of war material most pressing. And when we reflect upon the scarcity and inexperience of the workmen, and the great changes necessary in transforming an ordinary iron workshop into an arsenal in which all the machinery and tools had to be improvised, it is astonishing that so much was accomplished. The unfinished state of the vessel interfered so with the drills and exercises that we had but little opportunity of getting things into shape. It should be remembered that the ship was an experiment in naval architecture, differing in every respect from any then afloat. The officers and crew were strangers to the ship and to each other. Up to the hour of sailing she was crowded with workmen. Not a gun had been fired, hardly a revolution of the engines had been made, when we cast off from the dock and started on what many thought was an ordinary trial trip, but which proved to be a trial such as no vessel that ever floated had undergone up to that time. From the start we saw that she was slow, not over five knots; she steered so badly that, with her great length, it took from thirty to forty minutes to turn. She drew twenty-two feet, which confined us to a comparatively narrow channel in the Roads; and, as I have before said, the engines were our weak point. She was as unmanageable as a water-logged vessel.

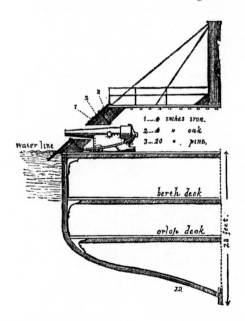

"Section of the 'Merrimac'" (*The Century Illustrated Monthly Magazine*, March 1885).

It was at noon on the 8th of March that we steamed down the Elizabeth River. Passing by our batteries, lined with troops, who cheered us as we passed, and through the obstructions at Craney Island, we took the south channel and headed for Newport News. At anchor at this time off Fort Monroe were the frigates *Minnesota*, *Roanoke*, and *St. Lawrence*, and several gun-boats. The first two were sister ships of the *Virginia* before the war; the last was a sailing frigate of fifty guns. Off Newport News, seven miles above, which was strongly fortified and held by a large Federal garrison, were anchored the frigate *Congress*, 50 guns, and the sloop *Cumberland*, 30. The day was calm, and the last two ships were swinging lazily by their anchors. (The tide was at its height about 1:40 P.M.) Boats were hanging to the lower booms, washed clothes in the rigging. Nothing indicated that we were expected; but when we came within three-quarters of a mile, the boats were dropped astern, booms got alongside, and the *Cumberland* opened with her heavy pivots, followed by the *Congress*, the gun-boats, and the shore batteries.

We reserved our fire until within easy range, when the forward pivot was pointed and fired by Lieutenant Charles Simms, killing and wounding most of the crew of the after pivot-gun of the *Cumberland*. Passing close to the *Congress*, which received our starboard broadside, and returned it with spirit, we steered direct for the *Cumberland*, striking her almost at right angles, under the fore-rigging on the starboard side. The blow was hardly perceptible on board the *Virginia*. Backing clear of her, we went ahead again, heading up the river, helm hard-a-starboard, and turned slowly. As we did so, for the first time I had an opportunity of using the

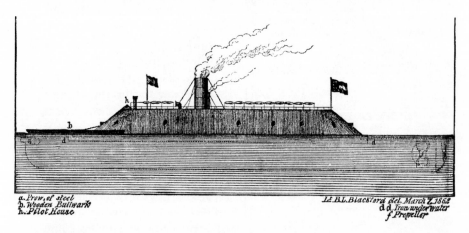

a. *Prow of steel*
b. *Wooden Bulwark*
h. *Pilot House*

Lt. B.L.Blackford del. March 7, 1862
d d. *Iron under water*
f *Propeller*

"The 'Merrimac,' from a sketch made the day before the fight" (*The Century Illustrated Monthly Magazine*, March 1885).

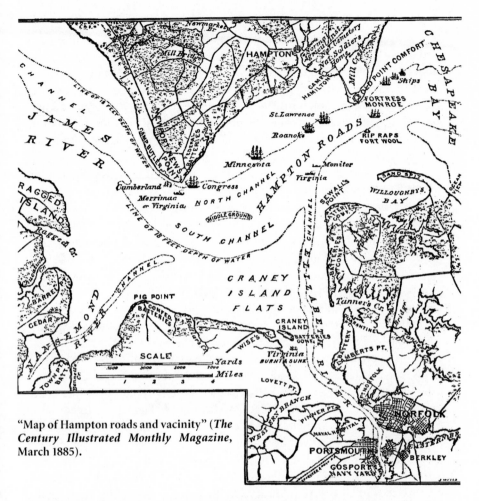

"Map of Hampton roads and vacinity" (*The Century Illustrated Monthly Magazine*, March 1885).

after-pivot of which I had charge. As we swung, the *Congress* came in range, nearly stern on, and we got in three raking shells. She had slipped her anchor, loosed her foretop-sail, run up the jib, and tried to escape, but grounded. Turning, we headed for her and took a position within two hundred yards, where every shot told. In the meantime the *Cumberland* continued the fight, though our ram had opened her side wide enough to drive in a horse and cart. Soon she listed to port and filled rapidly. The crew were driven by the advancing water to the spar-deck, and there worked her pivot-guns until she went down with a roar, the colors still flying. No ship was ever fought more gallantly. The *Congress* continued the unequal contest for more than an hour after the sinking of the *Cumberland*. Her losses were terrible, and finally she ran up the white flag.

As soon as we had hove in sight, coming down the harbor, the *Roanoke, St. Lawrence,* and *Minnesota,* assisted by tugs, had got under way, and started up from Old Point Comfort to join their consorts. They were under fire from the batteries at Sewell's Point, but the distance was too great to effect much. The first two, however, ran aground not far above Fort Monroe, and took but little part in the fight. The *Minnesota,* taking the middle or swash channel, steamed up half-way between Old Point Comfort and Newport News, when she grounded, but in a position to be actively engaged.

Previous to this we had been joined by the James River squadron, which had been at anchor a few miles above, and came into action most gallantly, passing the shore batteries at Newport News under a heavy fire, and with some loss. It consisted of the *Yorktown* (or *Patrick Henry*), 12 guns, Captain John R. Tucker; *Jamestown,* 2 guns, Lieut.-Commander J.N. Barney; and *Teaser,* 1 gun, Lieut.-Commander W.A. Webb.

As soon as the *Congress* surrendered, Commander Buchanan ordered the gun-boats *Beaufort,* Lieut.-Commander W.H. Parker, and *Raleigh,* Lieut.- Commander J.W. Alexander, to steam alongside, take off her crew, and set fire to the ship. Lieutenant Pendergrast, who had succeeded Lieutenant Smith, who had been killed, surrendered to Lieutenant Parker of the *Beaufort.* Delivering his sword and colors, he was directed by Lieutenant Parker to return to his ship and have the wounded transferred as rapidly as possible. All this time the shore batteries and small-arm men were keeping up an incessant fire on our vessels. Two of the officers of the *Raleigh,* Lieutenant Tayloe and Midshipman Hutter, were killed while assisting the Union wounded out of the *Congress.* A number of the enemy's men were killed by the same fire. Finally it became so hot that the gun-boats were obliged to haul off with only thirty prisoners, leaving Lieutenant Pendergrast and most of his crew on board, and they all afterward escaped to the shore by swimming or in small boats. While this was going on, the white flag was flying at her mainmast-head. Not being able to take possession of his prize, the commodore ordered hot shot to be used, and in a short time she was in flames fore and aft. While directing this, both himself and his flag-lieutenant, Minor, were severely wounded. The command then devolved upon Lieutenant Catesby Jones.

It was now 5 o'clock, nearly two hours of daylight, and the *Minnesota* only remained. She was aground and at our mercy. But the pilots would not attempt the middle channel with the ebb tide and approaching night. So we returned by the south channel to Sewell's Point and anchored, the *Minnesota* escaping, as we thought, only until morning.

Our loss in killed and wounded was twenty-one. The armor was hardly damaged, though at one time our ship was the focus on which were

"Commanders of the 'Merrimac'" (*left:* Commodore Franklin Buchanan, *right:* Commodore Josiah Tatnall) (*The Century Illustrated Monthly Magazine,* March 1885).

directed at least one hundred heavy guns, afloat and ashore. But nothing outside escaped. Two guns were disabled by having their muzzles shot off. The ram was left in the side of the *Cumberland*. One anchor, the smoke-stack, and the steam-pipes were shot away. Railings, stanchions, boat-davits, everything was swept clean. The flag-staff was repeatedly knocked over, and finally a boarding-pike was used. Commodore Buchanan and the other wounded were sent to the Naval Hospital, and after making preparations for the next day's fight, we slept at our guns, dreaming of other victories in the morning.

But at daybreak we discovered, lying between us and the *Minnesota*, a strange-looking craft, which we knew at once to be Ericsson's *Monitor*, which had long been expected in Hampton Roads, and of which, from different sources, we had a good idea. She could not possibly have made her appearance at a more inopportune time for us, changing our plans,

"The 'Merrimac' ramming the 'Cumberland'" (*The Century Illlustrated Monthly Magazine*, March 1885).

which were to destroy the *Minnesota*, and then the remainder of the fleet below Fort Monroe. She appeared but a pygmy compared with the lofty frigate which she guarded. But in her size was one great element of her success. I will not attempt a description of the *Monitor*; her build and peculiarities are well known.

After an early breakfast, we got under way and steamed out toward the enemy, opening fire from our bow pivot, and closing in to deliver our starboard broadside at short range, which was returned promptly from her 11-inch guns. Both vessels then turned and passed again still closer. The *Monitor* was firing every seven or eight minutes, and nearly every shot struck. Our ship

"Lieutenant George U. Morris, acting Commander of the 'Cumberland'" (*The Century Illustrated Monthly Magazine*, March 1885).

was working worse and worse, and after the loss of the smoke-stack, Mr. Ramsey, chief engineer, reported that the draught was so poor that it was with great difficulty that he could keep up steam. Once or twice the ship was on the bottom. Drawing 22 feet of water, we were confined to a narrow channel, while the *Monitor*, with only 12 feet immersion, could take any position, and always have us in range of her guns. Orders were given to concentrate our fire on the pilot-house, and with good result, as we afterward learned.[216] More than two hours had passed, and we had made no impression on the enemy so far as we could discover, while our wounds were slight. Several times the *Monitor* ceased firing, and we were in hopes she was disabled, but the revolution again of her turret and the heavy blows of her 11-inch shot on our sides soon undeceived us.

Coming down from the spar-deck, and observing a division standing "at ease," Lieutenant Jones inquired: "Why are you not firing, Mr. Eggleston?"

"Why, our powder is very precious," replied the lieutenant, "and after two hours' incessant firing I find that I can do her about as much damage by snapping my thumb at her every two minutes and a half."

Lieutenant Jones now determined to run her down or board her. For nearly an hour we manoeuvred for a position. Now "Go ahead!" now "Stop!" now "Astern!" The ship was as unwieldy as Noah's ark. At last an opportunity offered. "Go ahead, full speed!" But before the ship gathered headway, the *Monitor* turned, and our disabled ram only gave a glancing blow, effecting nothing. Again she came up on our quarter, her bow against our side, and at this distance fired twice. Both shots struck about half-way up the shield, abreast of the after pivot, and the impact forced the side in bodily two or three inches. All the crews of the after guns were knocked over by the concussion, and bled from the nose or ears. Another shot at the same place would have penetrated. While alongside, boarders were called away; but she dropped astern before they could get on board. And so, for six or more hours, the struggle was kept up. At length, the *Monitor* withdrew over the middle ground where we could not follow, but always maintaining a position to protect the *Minnesota*. To have run our ship ashore on a falling tide would have been ruin. We awaited her return for an hour; and at 2 o'clock P.M. steamed to Sewell's Point, and thence to the dockyard at Norfolk, our crew thoroughly worn out from the two days' fight. Although there is no doubt that the *Monitor* first retired—for Captain Van Brunt, commanding the *Minnesota*, so states in his official report—the battle was a drawn one, so far as the two vessels were concerned. But in its general results the advantage was with the *Monitor*. Our casualties in the second day's fight were only a few wounded.

This action demonstrated for the first time the power and efficiency of the ram as a means of offense. The side of the *Cumberland* was crushed like an egg-shell. The *Congress* and *Minnesota*, even with our disabled bow, would have shared the same fate but that we could not reach them on account of our great draught.

It also showed the power of resistance of two iron-clads, widely differing in construction, model, and armament, under a fire which in short time would have sunk any other vessel then afloat.

The *Monitor* was well handled, and saved the *Minnesota* and the remainder of the fleet at Fort Monroe. But her gunnery was poor. Not a single shot struck us at the water-line, where the ship was utterly unprotected, and where one would have been fatal. Or had the fire been concentrated on any one spot, the shield would have been pierced; or had larger charges been used, the result would have been the same. Most of her shot struck us obliquely, breaking the iron of both courses, but not

"The 'Merrimac' driving the 'Congress' from her anchorage" (*The Century Illustrated Monthly Magazine*, March 1885).

injuring the wood backing. When struck at right angles, the backing would be broken, but not penetrated. We had no solid projectiles, except a few of large windage, to be used as hot shot, and, of course, made no impression on the turret. But in all this it should be borne in mind that both vessels were on their trial trip, both were experimental, and both were receiving their baptism of fire.

On our arrival at Norfolk, Commodore Buchanan sent for me. I found him at the Naval Hospital, badly wounded and suffering greatly. He dictated a short dispatch to Mr. Mallory, Secretary of the Navy, stating the return of the ship and the result of the two days' fight, and directed me to proceed to Richmond with it and the flag of the *Congress*, and make a verbal report of the action, condition of the *Virginia*, etc.

I took the first train for Petersburg and the capital. The news had preceded me, and at every station I was warmly received, and to listening crowds was forced to repeat the story of the fight. Arriving at Richmond, I drove to Mr. Mallory's office and with him went to President Davis's,

"Escape of the crew of the 'Congress'" (*The Century Illustrated Monthly Magazine*, March 1885).

where we met Mr. Benjamin, who, a few days afterward, became Secretary of State, Mr. Seddon, afterward Secretary of War, General Cooper, Adjutant-General, and a number of others. I told at length what had occurred on the previous two days, and what changes and repairs were necessary to the *Virginia*. As to the future, I said that in the *Monitor* we had met our equal, and that the result of another engagement would be very doubtful. Mr. Davis made many inquiries as regarded the ship's draught, speed, and capabilities, and urged the completion of the repairs at as early a day as possible. The conversation lasted until near midnight. During the evening the flag of the *Congress*, which was a very large one, was brought in, and to our surprise, in unfolding it, we found it in some places saturated with blood. On this discovery it was quickly rolled up and sent to the Navy Department, where it remained during the war; it doubtless burned with that building when Richmond was evacuated.

The news of our victory was received everywhere in the South with the most enthusiastic rejoicing. Coming, as it did, after a number of disasters in the south and west, it was particularly grateful. Then again, under the circumstances, so little was expected from the navy that this success was entirely unlooked for. So, from one extreme to the other, the most extravagant anticipations were formed of what the ship could do. For instance: the blockade could be raised, Washington leveled to the ground, New York laid under contribution, and so on. At the North, equally groundless alarm was felt. As an example of this, Secretary Welles relates what took place at a Cabinet meeting called by Mr. Lincoln on the receipt of the news. "'The *Merrimac*,' said Stanton, 'will change the whole character of the war; she will destroy, *seriatim*, every naval vessel; she will lay all the cities on the seaboard under contribution. I shall immediately recall Burnside; Port Royal must be abandoned. I will notify the governors and municipal authorities in the North to take instant measures to protect their harbors.' He had no doubt, he said, that the monster was at this moment on her way to Washington; and, looking out the window, which commanded a view of the Potomac for many miles, 'Not unlikely, we shall have a shell or cannon-ball from one of her guns in the White House before we leave this room.' Mr. Seward, usually buoyant and self-reliant, overwhelmed with the intelligence, listened in responsive sympathy to Stanton, and was greatly depressed, as, indeed, were all the members."

I returned the next day to Norfolk, and informed Commodore Buchanan that he would be promoted to be admiral, and that, owing to his wound, he would be retired from the command of the *Virginia*. Lieutenant Jones should have been promoted, and should have succeeded him. He had fitted out the ship and armed her, and had commanded during the

"The explosion on the burning 'Congress'" (*The Century Illlustrated Monthly Magazine*, March 1885).

second day's fight. However, the department thought otherwise, and selected Commodore Josiah Tattnall; except Lieutenant Jones he was the best man. He had distinguished himself in the wars of 1812 and with Mexico. No one stood higher as an accomplished and chivalrous officer. While in command of the United States squadron in the East Indies, he was present as a neutral at the desperate fight at the Peiho Forts, below Pekin, between the English fleet and the Chinese, when the former lost nearly one-half of a force of twelve hundred engaged. Seeing his old friend Sir James Hope hard pressed and in need of assistance, having had four vessels sunk under him, he had his barge manned, and with his flag-lieutenant, S.D. Trenchard, pulled alongside the flag-ship, through the midst of tremendous fire, in which his coxswain was killed and several of his boat's crew were wounded. He found the gallant admiral desperately wounded, and all his crew killed or disabled but six. When he offered his services, surprise was expressed at his action. His reply was, "Blood is thicker than water."

Tattnall took command on the 29th of March. In the meantime the *Virginia* was in the dry dock under repairs. The hull four feet below the shield was covered with 2-inch iron. A new and heavier ram was strongly secured to the bow. The damage to the armor was repaired, wrought-iron port-shutters were fitted, and the rifle guns were supplied with steel-pointed solid shot. These changes, with 100 tons more of ballast on her fan-tails, increased her draught to 23 feet, improving her resisting powers, but correspondingly decreasing her mobility and reducing her speed to 4 knots. The repairs were not completed until the 4th of April, owing to our want of resources and the difficulty of securing workmen. On the 11th we steamed down the harbor to the Roads with six gun-boats, fully expecting to meet the *Monitor* again and other vessels; for we knew their fleet had been largely reënforced, by the *Vanderbilt*, among other vessels, a powerful side-wheel steamer fitted as a ram. We were primed for a desperate tussle; but to our surprise we had the Roads to ourselves. We exchanged a few shots with the Rip-Raps batteries, but the *Monitor* with the other vessels of the fleet remained below Fort Monroe, in Chesapeake Bay, where we could not get at them except by passing between the forts.

The day before going down, Commodore Tattnall had written to Secretary Mallory, "I see no chance for me but to pass the forts and strike elsewhere, and I shall be gratified by your authority to do so." This freedom of action was never granted, and probably wisely, for the result of an action with the *Monitor* and fleet, even if we ran the gauntlet of the fire of the forts successfully, was more than doubtful, and any disaster would have exposed Norfolk and James River, and probably would have resulted in the loss of Richmond. For equally good reasons the *Monitor* acted on the defensive; for if she had been out of the way, General

"Lieutenant Joseph B. Smith, acting-commander of the 'Congress'" (*Photograph by Black & Batchelder*) (*The Century Illlustrated Monthly Magazine*, March 1885).

McClellan's base and fleet of transports in York River would have been endangered. Observing three merchant vessels at anchor close inshore and within the bar at Hampton, the commodore ordered Lieutenant Barney in the *Jamestown* to go in and bring them out. This was promptly and successfully accomplished, under a fire from the forts. Two were brigs loaded with supplies for the army. The capture of these vessels, within gun-shot of their fleet, did not affect its movements. As the *Jamestown* towed her prizes under the stern of the English corvette *Rinaldo*, Captain Hewett (now [1887] Vice-Admiral Sir William Hewett, commanding the Channel Squadron), then at anchor in the Roads, she was enthusiastically cheered. We remained below all day, and at night returned and anchored off Sewell's Point.

A few days later we went down again to within gun-shot of the Rip-Raps, and exchanged a few rounds with the fort, hoping that the *Monitor* would come out of her lair into open water. Had she done so, a determined effort would have been made to carry her by boarding. Four small gun-boats were ready, each of which had its crew divided into parties for the performance of certain duties after getting on board. Some were to try to wedge the turret, some to cover the pilot-house and all the openings with tarpaulins, others to scale with ladders the turret and smoke-stack, using shells, hand-grenades, etc. Even if but two of the gun-boats should succeed in grappling her, we were confident of success. Talking this over since with Captain S.D. Greene, who was the first lieutenant of the *Monitor*, and in command after Captain Worden was wounded in the pilot-house, he said they were prepared for anything of this kind and that it would have failed. Certain it is, if an opportunity had been given, the attempt would have been made.

A break-down of the engines forced us to return to Norfolk. Having completed our

"Captain Ian Brunt, Commander of the 'Minnesota'" (*The Century Illustrated Monthly Magazine*, March 1885).

"The encounter at short range" (*The Century Illustrated Monthly Magazine*, March 1885).

repairs on May 8th, and while returning to our old anchorage, we heard heavy firing, and, going down the harbor, found the *Monitor*, with the iron-clads *Galena*, *Naugatuck*, and a number of heavy ships, shelling our batteries at Sewell's Point. We stood directly for the *Monitor*, but as we approached they all ceased firing and retreated below the forts. We followed close down to the Rip-Raps, whose shot passed over us, striking a mile or more beyond the ship. We remained for some hours in the Roads, and finally the commodore, in a tone of deepest disgust, gave the order: "Mr. Jones, fire a gun to windward, and take the ship back to her buoy."

During the month of April, 1862, our forces, under General J.E. Johnston, had retired from the Peninsula to the neighborhood of Richmond, to defend the city against McClellan's advance by way of the Peninsula, and from time to time rumors of the possible evacuation of Norfolk reached us. On the 9th of May, while at anchor off Sewell's Point, we noticed at sunrise that our flag was not flying over the batteries. A boat was sent ashore and found them abandoned. Lieutenant Pembroke Jones was then dispatched to Norfolk, some miles distant, to call upon General Huger, who was in command, and learn the condition of affairs. He returned during the afternoon, reporting, to our great surprise, the town deserted by our troops and the navy yard on fire. This precipitate retreat was entirely unnecessary, for while the *Virginia* remained afloat, Norfolk was safe, or, at all events, was not tenable by the enemy, and James River was partly guarded, for we could have retired behind the obstructions in the channel at Craney Island, and, with the batteries at that point, could have held the place, certainly until all the valuable stores and machinery had been removed from the navy yard. Moreover, had the *Virginia* been afloat at the time of the battles around Richmond, General McClellan would hardly have retreated to James River; for, had he done so, we could at any time have closed it and rendered any position on it untenable.

Norfolk evacuated, our occupation was gone, and the next thing to be decided upon was what should be done with the ship. Two courses of action were open to us: we might have run the blockade of the forts and done some damage to the shipping there and at the mouth of the York River, provided they did not get our of our way —for, with our great draught and low rate of speed, the enemy's transports would have gone where we could not have followed them; and the *Monitor* and other ironclads would have engaged us with every advantage, playing around us as rabbits around a sloth, and the end would have been the certain loss of the vessel. On the other hand, the pilots said repeatedly, if the ship were lightened to eighteen feet, they could take her up James River to Harrison's Landing or City Point, where she could have been put in fighting trim again, and have been in a position to assist in the defense of Richmond. The commodore decided upon this course. Calling all hands on deck, he told them what he wished done. Sharp and quick work was necessary; for, to be successful, the ship must be lightened five feet, and we must pass the batteries at Newport News and the fleet below before daylight next morning. The crew gave three cheers, and went to work with a will, throwing overboard the ballast from the fan-tails, as well as that below, — all spare stores, water, indeed everything but our powder and shot. By midnight the ship had been lightened three feet, when, to our amazement, the pilots said it was useless to do more, that with the westerly wind blowing, the tide would be cut down so that the ship would not go up even to Jamestown Flats; indeed, they would not take responsibility of taking her up the river at all. This extraordinary conduct of the pilots rendered some other plan immediately necessary. Moral: All officers, as far as possible, should learn to do their own piloting.

The ship had been so lifted as to be unfit for action; two feet of her hull below the shield was exposed. She could not be sunk again by letting in water without putting out the furnace fires and flooding the magazines. Never was a commander forced by circumstances over which he had no control into a more painful position than was Commodore Tattnall. But coolly and calmly he decided, and gave orders to destroy the ship; determining if he could not save his vessel, at all events not to sacrifice three hundred brave and faithful men; and that he acted wisely, the fight at Drewry's Bluff, which was the salvation of Richmond, soon after proved. She was run ashore near Craney Island, and the crew landed with their small-arms and two days' provisions. Having only two boats, it took three hours to disembark. Lieutenant Catesby Jones and myself were the last to leave. Setting her on fire fore and aft, she was soon in a blaze, and by the light of our burning ship we pulled for the shore, landing at daybreak. We marched 22 miles to Suffolk and took the cars for Richmond.

"The late commander Samuel Dana Greene, Executive Officer of the 'Monitor'" (*From a photograph during the war by Halleck, The Century Illustrated Monthly Magazine, March 1885*).

The news of the destruction of the *Virginia* caused a most profound feeling of disappointment and indignation throughout the South, particularly as so much was expected of the ship after our first success. On Commodore Tattnall the most unsparing and cruel aspersions were cast. He promptly demanded a court of inquiry, and, not satisfied with this, a court-martial, whose unanimous finding, after considering the facts and circumstances, was: "Being thus situated, the only alternative, in the opinion of the court, was to abandon and burn the ship then and there; which, in the judgment of the court, was deliberately and wisely done by order of the accused. Wherefore, the court do award the said Captain Josiah Tattnall an honorable acquittal."

It only remains now to speak of our last meeting with the *Monitor*. Arriving at Richmond, we heard that the enemy's fleet was ascending James River, and the result was great alarm; for, relying upon the *Virginia*, not a gun had been mounted to protect the city from a water attack. We were hurried to Drewry's Bluff, the first high ground below the city, seven miles distant. Here, for two days, exposed to constant rain, in bottomless mud and without shelter, on scant provisions, we worked unceasingly, mounting guns and obstructing the river. In this we were aided by the crews of small vessels which had escaped up the river before Norfolk was abandoned. The *Jamestown* and some small sailing-vessels were sunk in the channel, but, owing to the high water occasioned by a freshet, the obstructions were only partial. We had only succeeded in getting into position three thirty-twos and two sixty-fours (shell guns) and were without sufficient supply of ammunition, when on the 15th of May the iron-clad *Galena*, Commander John Rodgers, followed by the *Monitor* and three others, hove in sight. We opened fire as soon as they came within range, directing most of it on the *Galena*. This vessel was handled very skillfully. Coming up within six hundred yards of the battery, she anchored, and with a spring from her quarter, presented her broadside; this under a heavy fire, and in a narrow river with a strong current.

The *Monitor*, and others anchored just below, answered our fire deliberately; but, owing to the great elevation of the battery, their fire was in a great measure, ineffectual, though two guns were dismounted and several men were killed and wounded. While this was going on, our sharp-shooters were at work on both banks. Lieutenant Catesby Jones, in his report, speaks of this service: "Lieutenant Wood, with a portion of the men, did good service as sharp-shooters. The enemy were excessively annoyed by their fire. His position was well chosen and gallantly maintained in spite of the shell, shrapnel, grape, and canister fired at them." Finding they could make no impression on our works, the *Galena*, after an action of four hours, returned down river with her consorts. Her losses were about forty killed and wounded.

This was one of the boldest and best-conducted operations of the war, and one of which very little notice has been taken. Had Commander Rodgers been supported by a few brigades, landed at City Point or above on the south side, Richmond would have been evacuated. The *Virginia's* crew alone barred his way to Richmond; otherwise the obstructions would not have prevented his steaming up to the city, which would have been as much at his mercy as was New Orleans before the fleet of Farragut.

It should be remembered that as spring opened General McClellan was urged by the administration and press to make a forward movement. Anticipating this, General J.E. Johnston, better to cover Richmond and to shorten his lines, retired to the Rappahannock and later to the James. General McClellan wisely determined to use the navigable waters either of the James or the York River to approach Richmond; and as the James was closed by the *Virginia* in a manner he could not have foreseen, he was forced to use the York as his base of action against Richmond—a circumstance that saved the city from capture for three years.

The engagement at Drewry's Bluff or Fort Darling, as it is sometimes called, was the last service of the *Virginia's* crew as a body; soon after they were scattered among the different vessels at Southern ports. The *Monitor*, too, disappeared from sight a few months later, foundering off Cape Hatteras while on a voyage to Charleston. So short-lived were the two vessels that revolutionized the navies of the world.

Chapter 9

The *Tallahassee's* Dash
into New York Waters

Wood's first published article on his service in 1864 as the com-
mander of the Confederate cruiser CSS Tallahassee *(formerly the*
blockade runner Atalanta*) was the memoir "Running the Blockade at*
Halifax," which appeared in the Halifax Carnival Echo *in 1889*
(5–10 August). Almost a decade later, he prepared a second, revised
account of the Tallahassee's cruise, "A Cruise on a Blockade Runner,"
which was delivered as a paper to the Philomathic Society of Dal-
housie College on 11 February 1898 (a portion of the paper appeared
in Halifax's The Evening Mail *on 14 February 1898 and in* The Halifax Herald *on 15 February 1898).*

"The Tallahassee's *Dash into New York Waters" was Wood's third*
version of the story. Presented as the first of two pieces devoted to "Con-
federate Commerce-Destroyers" in the July 1898 issue of The Century
Illustrated Monthly Magazine, *it provides what is probably the best*
description of the warship's voyage, including her daring escape from
Halifax through the dangerous Eastern Passage. It is this version which
is reprinted verbatim here. (In 1959, an abridged version of the text
appeared in Philip Van Doren Stern's Secret Missions of the Civil War.
The full memoir was reprinted in 1987 as part of an obscure pamphlet
series issued by the small-press publisher Robert Hardy Publications of
Suffolk, Virginia [see Appendix 4]).

While excerpts from the account no longer appear, as they once
did, in school readers in Nova Scotia, a school near Wood's escape
route has been named in honor of his vessel.[217] *However, during the*
past decade, several Nova Scotian researchers have questioned the
accuracy of Wood's account of his departure from Halifax (see, for

instance, the items by David Harris and David Sutherland listed in the annotated bibliography), noting that the historical record indicates that Union naval vessels actually arrived at Halifax after the Tallahassee had left. Furthermore, it has even been suggested that Wood did not in fact use the Eastern Passage as his route out of Halifax harbor.

While it is very probable that Union warships did reach Halifax after Wood had made good his escape, this fact hardly detracts from his achievement. Wood had every reason to believe that the Northern naval forces were waiting for him, and he acted accordingly. As for other aspects of his account, it should be noted that not only was Wood's version corroborated by the pilot Jock Flemming, but many details can also be verified in official records and contemporary newspaper accounts. Moreover, given his eventful — and well-documented — military career during the Civil War, it seems unlikely that Wood, who was noted for his modesty, would feel compelled to embellish the story of his escape from Halifax, as it was hardly his sole — or even main — claim to fame.

As Wood notes in the conclusion of his memoir, after he left the Tallahassee the vessel (renamed CSS Olustee) made one more cruise as a raider. She was then converted to the blockade runner CSS Chameleon and placed under the command of Captain John Wilkinson (whom Wood mentions in his narrative). Sent to Bermuda from Wilmington, North Carolina, near the end of 1864, she was unable to re-enter a Southern port and was forced to cross the Atlantic to Liverpool, arriving the day of Robert E. Lee's surrender at Appomattox on 9 April 1865. Seized by the British, the vessel was turned over to the United States and renamed the Amelia. Sold to the Japanese in 1867, she sailed as the merchantman Haya Maru until 17 June 1869, when she sank while en route to Hioge-Kobe from Yokohoma.

As for John Wilkinson, the vessel's last Confederate commander, he eventually made his way from England to Halifax, where he was, for a time, John Taylor Wood's partner in the firm Wilkinson, Wood and Company.

For a full listing of the thirty-three vessels captured by the Tallahassee during her nineteen-day voyage out of Wilmington in August 1864, see Appendix 2. While Wood's successful raiding served to boost Southern morale, it also resulted in the tightening of the blockade at Wilmington, the Confederacy's last important source of supply.

The engravings which accompany the article are taken from Century magazine.

THE *TALLAHASSEE'S* DASH
INTO NEW YORK WATERS

From the capes of the Chesapeake to the mouth of the Rio Grande is a coastline over three thousand miles; and, as the blockade began at Washington on the Potomac, if we include the inland waters of Virginia, North Carolina, and other states, this distance is doubled. It was this long stretch of coast, fronting on nine states, that by proclamation of President Lincoln was placed under blockade in the spring of 1861. The means of making it effective were inadequate. The navy of the United States, comprising some forty vessels, was distributed on different stations in every part of the world. Not more than five or six steamers were immediately available. However, a navy was rapidly improvised by the purchase or charter of a large number of steamers of all kinds and classes, from a ferry-boat to a Liverpool steam-packet; and in the course of a few months the principal points were covered; but not as they were later, when, during the last years of the war, a larger number of vessels were employed in blockading Wilmington or Charleston than were used on the whole coast during the first year. Independent of the men-of-war built at the Union navy-yards, nearly 500 vessels, principally steamers, were taken from the merchant service and converted into cruisers.

As great as was the extent of the Confederate coast, but comparatively few points had to be guarded. From Cape Henry to Wilmington there was but one harbor that could be used — that of Beaufort, which was soon occupied by the Federals. The inlets and sounds of the Carolinas, Georgia, and the Gulf States, which were easily accessible, were not used by the blockade-runners, for they had no connections with the interior, and no facilities for handling cargoes. And even the few ports that could be entered were rapidly lessened by occupation, both in the Gulf and the Atlantic; so that after the second year of the war but two ports— Wilmington and Charleston — were open to the Confederacy.

It was through these that the Confederates continued to receive supplies of all kinds to within a few months of the close of the war. Both were difficult to approach on account of the shoals which obstruct their harbors, and for the same reason it was difficult to blockade them effectually. With the occupation of Morris Island, and the closing of all channels but one leading to Charleston, Wilmington became the favorite resort. This town is situated on Cape Fear River, about thirty miles above its two entrances into the Atlantic. Fronting the mouth of the river is Smith's Island and Frying-Pan Shoals, extending seaward some eighteen miles. Though the two entrances are only six miles apart, the distance by sea is

"Night Escape of the 'Tallahassee' off Wilmington" (*The Century Illustrated Monthly Magazine,* July 1898).

some forty miles, and each required a distinct blockading squadron. The access to both was hazardous on account of shoals, shifting in position and depth of water with every heavy gale. The western inlet was guarded by Fort Caswell, an ante-bellum work. The eastern or new inlet was protected by Fort Fisher, a very formidable earthwork with outlying defenses.

On either flank and in front of the Atlantic coast of the United States are the English stations of Halifax, Nassau, and Bermuda. The last two were the main feeders of the blockade. Nassau, on one of the Bahamas, is six hundred miles south of Wilmington, and Bermuda seven hundred miles east. Both can be approached from every direction, and afforded safe and hospitable ports for the blockade-runners. Halifax, eight hundred miles to the northward and eastward, was used only occasionally. At the outset steamers, and even sailing vessels, were used for this trade; but as the stringency of the blockade increased, steamers better fitted for the work were employed, and finally a class especially adapted to the service was built in England. They were long, low, lightly constructed iron steamers of light draft, with powerful motive power, either screw or feathered paddle-wheels, with no spars, and were painted lead-color.

The captain of a successful blockade-runner needed to be a thorough seaman and a skilful navigator. His work required boldness, decision in emergencies, and the faculty of commanding and inspiring the confidence of his crew. There were captains who ran in and out a great number of times. Captain John Wilkinson made twenty-one successful runs inside of twelve months, and not in a fast steamer. That absence of these qualities would invite loss was made apparent in a great number of instances, when the steamers were almost thrown away by bad landfalls, or by the captain or crew wilting at the first sight of a cruiser or the sound of a gun. The pecuniary stake was large; and blockade-running offered a certain amount of excitement and adventure that drew into its service some distinguished foreign naval officers, who, under their own or assumed names, made the most successful commanders.

Among the steamers coming to Wilmington I had long been on the lookout for a suitable one which would answer for a cruiser, and finally selected the *Atlanta*, an iron twin-screw of seven hundred tons gross, and two hundred feet long.[218] She had been built at Millwall, below London, ostensibly for the Chinese opium trade; and was a first-class, well-constructed vessel, and fast, making fourteen and a quarter knots on her trial trip. She had two engines, which could be worked together or separately. The necessary changes were soon made to receive the crew and armament. The latter consisted of one rifled 100-pounder amidships, one rifled, 60-hundredweight 32-pounder forward, and one long Parrott aft. The officers and crew were all volunteers from the Confederate gunboats on the James River and North Carolina waters. She was formally put in commission on July 20, 1864, and rechristened the *Tallahassee*.

My orders from the Secretary of the Navy were general in their scope. "The character and force of your vessel," they said, "point to the enemy's commerce as the most appropriate field of action, and the existing blockade of our ports constrains the destruction of our prizes."

Ten days sufficed to get things in working order, and the crew into shape, when we dropped down the river to wait a favorable time for running the gantlet, which was only when there was no moon and when the tide served. I determined to try the eastern, or new, inlet, and on the night of August 4 the outlook was favorable. Everything was secured for sea. The lights were all carefully housed, except the binnacle, which was shaded; fires were cleaned and freshened, lookouts were stationed, and the men were at their quarters. The range lights were placed; these, in the absence of all buoys and lights, were necessary in crossing the bar, and were shown only when vessels were going in and out. The Mound, a huge earthwork, loomed up ahead, looking in the darkness like a black cloud resting on the horizon. We started ahead slowly, but brought up on the "rip," or inner shoal. Two hours of hard work with the engines, and with a kedge astern, were lost before we got off, and then it was too late for the tide. We turned up the river a short distance, and anchored. The next night we had the same experience, except that we grounded so badly that it required three steamers to tow us off.

Finding that with the state of the tide and our thirteen and a half feet draft the eastern inlet was impracticable, I determined to try the western one. Steaming down to Fort Caswell, we waited for darkness. Only a few fleeting clouds were in the sky. As the moon went down on the night of August 6, at ten, we approached the bar, fearful of a repetition of our previous mishaps; and as the leadsman called out the water in a low tone, our hearts rose in our throats as it shoaled: "By the mark three — a quarter less three — and a half two — and a quarter two." She touched, but did not bring up. Then came the joyful words: "And a half two."

We had just grazed the "Lump," a bad shoal in mid-channel, and were over the bar. Chief Engineer Tynan was by my side on the bridge. I turned to him and said: "Open her out, sir, but let her go for all she is worth." With a bound he was in the engine-room, and in a few moments I knew from the tremor of the vessel that the order was obeyed, and with a full head of steam we leaped on. "A sharp lookout ahead!" was the order passed forward. We were hardly clear of the bar when back came the words: "A steamer on the starboard bow!" "A steamer ahead!" The two made us out at the same time, and signaled. I hailed the forecastle, and asked how the steamer under our bows was heading. "To the southward," was the reply. The helm was accordingly ported, and we passed between them, so close under the stern of the one that was ahead that a biscuit could have been tossed on board. As we dashed by we heard the sharp, quick words of command of the officer in charge of the after pivot: "Run out!" "Starboard tackle handsomely!" "Elevate!" "Steady!" "Stand clear!" Then the flash from the muzzle, like a gleam of lightning, illumined the water for a moment, and a heavy shell flew singing over our heads, leaving a trail like a comet. It was an excellent line shot. That order, "Elevate!" had saved us. The steamer on the starboard side opened, and our opponents, now on our quarter, joined in; but their practice was wild, and in a few moments they were out of sight. I did not return their fire, for it would only have shown our position, and I did not want our true character to be known, preferring that they should suppose us an ordinary blockade-runner.

During the night we ran to the southward until clear of Frying-Pan Shoals, and then hauled up to the eastward. More to be feared than the inshore squadron were the vessels cruising offshore from forty to fifty miles, in a position to sight at daylight the vessels that might come out during the night, and these were the fastest and most efficient blockaders.

I was not surprised when, at daylight the next morning, a cruiser was reported in sight astern, hull up. As we were outlined against the eastern sky, she had seen us first, and from the dense smoke issuing from her funnel I knew she was in sharp chase. At eight another steamer was made out ahead. I changed our course eight points, bringing one on each beam, and the chase became interesting. One we made out to be a large side-wheeler, and she held her own, if she did not gain. Mr. Tynan made frequent visits to the engine-room, trying to coax out a few more revolutions; and he succeeded, for we brought them gradually on our quarter, and by noon had lowered their hulls two or three strakes. It was at times like this that the ship and engines proved themselves reliable; for had a screw loosened or a journal heated we should have been lost.

The ship was very deep with an extra supply of coal, and probably out of trim, so we were prepared, if hard pressed, to sacrifice some of it. Fortunately it was calm, and they could not use their canvas to help them. It was Sunday, and feeling relieved as to our pursuers, all hands were called, and divine service was read. By 4 PM our pursuers were astern, hull down, and had evidently given up. About the same time another was sighted from the masthead; but by changing our course a few points she was kept at a respectful distance. Just after dark we were nearly on top of another before we could change our course. Burning a blue light, the stranger headed for us. As we did not answer her signal, it was repeated, and a minute later she opened fire. The shells passed uncomfortably near, but in a half-hour we lost sight of each other in the darkness. The fact that we were chased by four cruisers on our first day out proved how effective was the blockade. Upward of fifty vessels were employed at this time outside the port of Wilmington — vessels, of all kinds, from the 40-gun frigate to the captured tin-plate blockade-runner — a larger number than were ever before employed on like service at one port.

The next few days were uneventful. We stood to the northward and eastward, under easy steam, and spoke several English and foreign vessels, from one of which we got late New York papers. Twenty miles below Long Branch we made our first prize, the schooner *Sarah A. Boyce* of Boston, for Philadelphia in ballast. Her crew and their personal effects were brought on board, and she was scuttled. In all cases the prisoners were allowed to retain a bag of their clothes; nor were they asked for their money, watches, etc. In one case it was reported to me that one of the crew had taken a watch from a prisoner; this being found to be true, it was returned, and the man was punished. The chronometers, charts, and medicine-chests were the only things taken out of the prizes, except such provisions as were necessary.

Standing over toward Fire Island Light, on the Long Island shore, we found seven sail in sight. One ran down toward us, which we recognized at once as a New York pilot-boat. She luffed to under our quarter, launched a small boat, and a few minutes later a large, well-dressed man in black, with a high hat, heavy gold watch-guard, a small valise, and a bundle of papers under his arm, stepped over the side. As he did so his eyes glanced up at our flag at the peak, which was lazily unfolding in a light breeze.

"My —! what is that? What ship is this?" said he, turning to me.

"The Confederate cruiser *Tallahassee*," I replied.

A more astonished man never stood on deck of vessel. He turned deadly pale, and drops of perspiration broke from every pore; but rapidly bracing himself, he took in the situation, and prepared to make the best of it. He was told that his vessel was a prize, and that I would make a tender of her. He was ordered to go on board, and return with his crew and their personal effects. It was the pilot-boat *James Funk*, No. 22, one of a class of fine weatherly schooners found off New York, from one or two hundred miles out, at all seasons, manned by as thorough seamen as ever trod ship's deck. Years before, while attached to the sloop of war *Germantown*, I had seen one of them work this vessel under sail down the East River, against a head wind but fair tide, "backing and filling" in a manner that called forth the admiration of all. I put on board two officers and twenty men, with orders to keep within signal distance. She was very efficient when several sail were in sight, overhauling and bringing alongside vessels, that I might decide upon their fate. The captures of the bark *Bay State* and the brigs *Carrie Estelle* and *A. Richards* followed in quick succession. We had now over forty prisoners and their baggage on board, lumbering up our decks, and it was necessary to make some disposition of them. Toward night No. 22 brought alongside the schooner *Carroll*. She was bonded by the captain, acting for the owners, for ten thousand dollars; and after he had given a written engagement to land the prisoners at New York, they went on board with their effects. Before leaving they were all paroled. All the prisoners we made, with hardly an exception, were most eager for their paroles. One said: "This is worth three hundred and fifty dollars to me." "I would not take a thousand dollars for mine," said another. One skipper said that if it would protect him from the draft he was partly reconciled to the loss of his vessel. Another, whose vessel had been bonded, brought all his crew on board to secure their papers.

The next victim was another pilot-boat, the *William Bell*, No. 24. My object in capturing these vessels was, if possible, to secure a pilot who could either be paid or coerced to take the ship through Hell Gate into Long Island Sound. It was now near the full moon. It was my intention to

"The 'Tallahassee' chasing the pilot-boat 'William Bell'" (*The Century Illustrated Monthly Magazine*, July 1898).

run up the harbor just after dark, as I knew the way in by Sandy Hook, then to go on up the East River, setting fire to the shipping on both sides, and when abreast of the navy-yard to open fire, hoping some of our shells might set fire to the buildings and any vessels that might be at the docks, and finally to steam through Hell Gate into the Sound. I knew from the daily papers, which we received only a day or two old, what vessels were in port, and that there was nothing then ready that could oppose us. But no pilot could be found who knew the road, or who was willing to undertake it, and I was forced to abandon the scheme.

From these inquiries arose the report that I would attempt to enter the harbor. Three days were spent between the light-ship and Montauk Point, sometimes within thirty miles of the former — and about twenty prizes were taken. The most important was the packetship *Adriatic*, one thousand tons, from London, with a large and valuable cargo and one hundred and seventy passengers. On account of the latter I was afraid I would have to bond the ship; but fortunately our tender came down before the wind, convoying the bark *Suliote*, and I determined to use her as a cartel after the captain had given bonds for ten thousand dollars. She was laden with coal; but the distance to Sandy Hook was only seventy miles. The passengers were nearly all Germans, and when told their ship was to be burned were terribly alarmed; and it was some time before they could comprehend that we did not intend to burn them also. Three hours were occupied in transferring them and their effects with our boats. In many cases they insisted upon taking broken china, bird-cages, straw beds, and the most useless articles, leaving their valuables behind. After all were safely on board the *Suliote*, the *Adriatic* was fired; and as night came on the burning ship illuminated the waters for miles, making a picture of rare beauty. The breeze was light and tantalizing, so our tender was taken in tow, and we steamed slowly to the eastward toward Nantucket. The neighborhood of New York had been sufficiently worked, and the game was alarmed and scarce.

Rounding South Shoal light-ship, we stood in toward Boston Bay. As the tender proved a drawback to our rapid movements, I determined to destroy her. It was a mistake, for I was authorized by the government to fit out any prize as a cruiser, and this one ought to have been sent along the eastern coast. A number of sail were sighted, but most of them were foreigners; this could be told by the "cut of their jibs." It was not necessary to speak them. A few unimportant captures were made, and then we sighted a large bark. First Lieutenant Ward, the boarding officer, returned, and reported the *Glenarvon*, Captain Watt, a fine new vessel of Thomaston, Maine, from Glasgow with iron. He was ordered to return and secure the nautical instruments, etc., and scuttle her, and bring on board the prisoners. The captain had his wife on board, and as passengers another captain returning home with his wife — an elderly pair. We watched the bark as she slowly settled, strake by strake, until her deck was awash, and then her stern sank gradually out of sight until she was in an upright position, and one mast after another disappeared with all sail set, sinking as quietly as if human hands were lowering her into the depths. Hardly a ripple broke the quiet waters. Her head spars were the last seen. Captain Watt and his wife never took their eyes off their floating home, but side by side, with tears in their eyes, watched her disappear. "Poor fellow," she said afterward, "he has been going to sea for thirty years, and all our savings were in that ship. We were saving for our dear children at home —five of them."

Miserable business is war, ashore or afloat. A brave, true, and gentle woman, at the same time strong in her conviction of what she thought right, was the captain's wife, and she soon won the admiration and respect of all on board. But what shall I say of the passenger and his wife? If I said she was the very reverse of the above, it would not begin to do her justice. She came on board scolding, and left scolding. Her tongue was slung amidships, and never tired. Her poor husband, patient and meek as the patriarch, came in for his full share. Perhaps the surroundings and the salt air acted as an irritant, for I can hardly conceive of this cataract of words poured on a man's head on shore without something desperate happening. Even Mrs. Watt did not escape for quietly criticizing President Lincoln and his conduct of the war, particularly as regards the navy, on which point she could speak feelingly; Xantippe even threatened to report her to the police as soon as they reached the United States.[219] At rare intervals there was a calm, and then she employed the time in distributing tracts and Testaments. When she left us to take passage in a Russian bark, she called down on us all the imprecations that David showered on his

"The sinking of the bark 'Glenarvon'" (*The Century Illustrated Monthly Magazine*, July 1898).

enemies. And as a final effort to show how she would serve us, she snatched her bonnet from her head, tore it in pieces, and threw it into the sea. Peace to her memory! I gave them my cabin; indeed, from the time of leaving Wilmington I had but little use of it. I slept and lived on the bridge or in the chart-room, hardly taking off my clothes for weeks.

We ran along the eastern coast as far as Matinicus, Maine, but over-hauled nothing of importance, only passing a large number of small fishing-craft and coasters. One night a large steamer, heavily sparred, passed within musket-shot, but did not see us. Her lights were in sight for an hour, but we showed none. Steering to the eastward round Seal Island and Cape Sable Island, the western extremity of Nova Scotia, we, of course, had our share of the "ever-brooding, all-concealing fog" which in the summer season is a fixed quantity in this neighborhood. Suddenly, one evening, the fog lifted, and we discovered a ship close aboard. Pass-ing under her stern, we read *James Littlefield* of Bangor. Hailing the cap-tain, and asking him where from, and where bound, "From Cardiff, with coals for New York," came back as his answer. He was told to heave to. Here was the cargo of all others that we wanted, and I determined to uti-lize it, if possible. Lieutenant Ward was sent on board to take charge, put her under easy sail, and keep within one or two cable-lengths of the steamer. As the night closed in the fog became denser than ever, so much so that one end of the vessel could not be seen from the other — a gen-uine Bay of Fundy fog, one that could be handled. For some hours, by blowing our whistle every five minutes, while the ship was ringing a bell, we kept within sound of each other. But the latter gradually grew duller, until we lost it altogether; and I spent an anxious night, fearing that should it continue thick we might be separated. But soon after sunrise a rift in the fog, disclosing a small sector of the horizon, showed us the ship some five miles away. Steaming alongside, I determined to take no more risks in the fog. Banking our fires, we passed a hawser from our bows to the ship's quarter, and let her tow us. I held on to the ship, hoping it would become smooth enough to lay the two vessels alongside and take out a supply of coals; for although there was only a moderate breeze, there was an old sea running from the south'ard. To use our boats would have been an endless and dangerous operation. I thought of taking her into one of the small outposts on the neighboring coast of Nova Scotia; but this would have been a clear case of violation of neutral territory. The day passed without change in weather or sea, and very reluctantly I was compelled to abandon the hope of free coals, and look to Halifax for a supply. Ordering Lieutenant Ward to scuttle the ship, we left her to be a home for the cod and lobster.

After being two or three days without observations and without a departure, to find your port in a thick fog requires a sharp lookout and a constant use of the lead. However, we made a good hit. The first "land" we made was the red head of a fisherman, close under our bows, in a small boat, who in the voice of a Boanerges, and in words more forcible than complimentary, warned us against tearing his nets.[220] In answer to our inquiries in regard to the bearings of Sambro, Chebucto Head, etc., he offered to pilot the ship in. Accepting his services, and taking his boat in tow, we stood up the harbor. Soon we emerged from the fog, and the city of Halifax was in sight.

The harbor of Halifax is well known as safe, commodious, easy of access, and offering many advantages. Coming to anchor, I had my gig manned, and went on board the line-of-battle ship *Duncan*, to call upon Sir James Hope, commanding on this station, and then upon the governor, Sir Richard Graves MacDonnell, who received me very kindly, asking me to breakfast next morning, a compliment which I was obliged to decline, owing to the limited time at my disposal. By the Queen's proclamation, the belligerents could use her ports only for twenty-four hours, except in case of distress, and take no supplies, except sufficient to reach the nearest home port. I wanted only coal, and by the energetic action of our agents, Messrs. B. Wier & Co., I was able to procure a supply of the best Welsh.[221] To a distinguished gentleman of the medical profession we were indebted for a new spar; for I neglected to mention that while off New York we were in collision with the ship *Adriatic*, and lost our mainmast and all attached.[222]

From the time of our arrival, Judge Jackson, the energetic American consul, had not ceased to bombard the authorities, both civil and military, with proofs, protests, and protocols in regard to our ship. He alleged general misdemeanours, that we had violated all the rules of war, and protested against our taking in supplies. The provincial government acted as a buffer, and I heard of the protests only in a modified form. However, I was anxious to conform to the Queen's mandate, and could only plead our partly disabled condition for exceeding the twenty-four hours. To my request for an additional twelve hours I received the following answer:

> Government House, Halifax, N.S.,
> 19th August, 1864.
>
> Sir: In reply to your application for additional time to ship a main mast, I have no objection to grant it, as I am persuaded that I can rely on your not taking any unfair advantage of the indulgence which I concede. I do so the more readily because I find that you have not attempted to ship

more than the quantity of coals necessary for your immediate use. I have, etc.,

(Signed) Richard G. MacDonnell
Lieut.-Governor.

Com. J. Taylor Wood, C.S. Cruiser Tallahassee

In writing to Mr. Cardwell, Secretary of State for the Colonies, on the 23d of August, the lieutenant-governor said:

> It was clear that a cruiser reported to have captured or destroyed between thirty or forty vessels in about twelve days, and said to have speed exceeding by five knots that of the Alabama, was the most formidable adversary which Federal commerce had yet encountered. Under these circumstances, if she was permitted to take in a supply of coal here in excess of that strictly allowed, I felt that I should be enabling her to use one of her Majesty's ports for the purpose of procuring the material most destructive to the shipping and property of a power with which her Majesty is at peace. In the peculiar case of the Tallahassee, every five tons of coal in excess of the amount strictly allowable might be regarded as insuring heavy loss to Federal shipping. Accordingly, when Captain Wood applied later in the day for permission to complete his complement of coals up to one hundred tons, I informed him that he was at liberty to do so, and expressed my gratification at finding that he had not been using the extra period of his stay for the purpose of obtaining more coals than sufficed for his immediate wants. I also, in communicating that permission to the admiral, requested the latter to relieve Captain Wood from further surveillance, as I was extremely anxious, under the circumstances, to avoid wounding his feelings. Later in the day he applied for, and I gave him, permission to remain twelve hours longer for the purpose of shipping a new main mast. He did not, however, wholly avail himself of that permission; for without waiting to step the mast, he left the harbor soon after midnight, as appears from the inclosed full and satisfactory report obligingly transmitted to me by the admiral.

At the close of the second day our new mast was towed alongside and hoisted in. Immediate preparations were made for sea. During the day two or more of the enemy's cruisers were reported off the harbor; indeed, one came in near enough to communicate with the shore. During our stay we had seen late New York papers with accounts of our cruise, and the excitement it had caused on the seaboard. The published reports of most of the prisoners were highly colored and sensational. We were described in anything but complimentary terms. A more blood-thirsty or piratical-looking crew never sailed, according to some narratives. Individually I plead guilty; for three years of rough work, with no chance of replenishing my wardrobe, had left me in the plight of Major Dalgetty.[223] When I called upon the admiral I had to borrow a make-up from some of the ward-room officers.

"The 'Tallahassee' burning the packet 'Adriatic'" (*The Century Illustrated Monthly Magazine*, July 1898).

We noticed that a number of vessels had been sent in pursuit. A Washington telegram said: "The first information of the depredations of the *Tallahassee* was received by the Navy Department on the 12th instant, after office hours. Secretary Welles immediately ordered the following vessels in pursuit: namely, *Juniata, Susquehanna, Eolus, Pontoosuc, Dumbarton,* and *Tristram Shandy,* on the 13th; the *Moccasin, Aster, Yantic, R.R. Cuyler,* and *Grand Gulf* on the 14th; and on the 15th the *Dacotah* and *San Jacinto.* These were all the vessels available in the navy."

It began to look as though we would have to run the blockade again. To my request to Mr. Wier for a good pilot, he sent on board Jock Flemming. He was six feet in height, broad, deep-chested, and with a stoop. His limbs were too long for his body. His head was pitched well forward, and covered, as was his neck, with a thick stubble of grayish hair. His eyes were small and bright, beneath overhanging eyebrows. His hands were as hard, rough, and scaly as the flipper of a green turtle. Bronzed by exposure to sixty seasons of storm and sunshine, he could tell of many a narrow escape, carrying on to keep offshore in a northeast snow-storm, or trying to hold on in a howling nor'wester, when every drop of water that came on board was congealed into ice, and soon the vessel was little better than an iceberg, and nothing remained but to run off into the Gulf

Stream to thaw out. He knew the harbor as well as the fish that swam its waters. He was honest, bluff, and trusty.

MacNab's Island divides the entrance to the harbor of Halifax into two channels. The main, or western, one is broad, deep, and straight, and is the only one used, except by small coasters. The eastern is just the reverse, without buoys or lights. In looking over the chart with Flemming, I asked him if it was not possible to go out through the latter passage, and so avoid the enemy lying off the mouth of the main channel. I saw only five or six feet marked on the chart over the shoalest spot at low water.

"How much do you draw, cap'?"

"Thirteen feet, allowing for a little drag."

"There is a good tide to-night, and water enough; but you are too long to turn the corners."

"But, pilot, with our twin-screws, I can turn her around on her center, as I turn this ruler."

"Well, I never was shipmate with the likes of them; but if you will steer her, I'll find the water."

"Are you certain, pilot, there is water enough? It would never do to run ashore at this time."

"You sha'n't touch anything but the eel-grass. Better get ready about eleven."

I hesitated; and divining from my face that I was not satisfied, he said as he rose: "Don't be 'feared; I'll take you out all right; you won't see any of those chaps off Chebucto Head."

As he spoke he brought his hand down on my shoulder with a thud that I felt in my boots. His confidence, and my faith in the man, determined me to make the attempt. Some friends and English officers were on board to the last; and as we hove up the anchor and started ahead at midnight, they left us with hearty good wishes. The moon was old and waning with dark clouds rapidly chasing one another across its face from the southward. Steaming slowly out, only the dark shores of MacNab's Island on one side and the mainland on the other could be seen, but whether a stone's throw or a mile distant could not be discovered. Once or twice Flemming appeared lost, but it was only for a moment. At the sharp twists in the channel I sent a boat ahead with a light to mark the turns. At one place, by the lead, there was hardly room between the keel and the bottom for your open hand. In an hour we opened the two lights on Devil's Island, and the channel broadened and deepened. Soon we felt the pulsating bosom of the old Atlantic, and were safe outside, leaving our waiting friends miles to the westward. Flemming dropped his boat alongside, and with a hearty shake of the hand, and an earnest God-speed, swung himself into it, and was soon lost in the darkness. He had kept his word, bringing us out without feeling the bottom — a real achievement. Years after I often met him, and there was nothing in the old man's life he was so fond of relating as how he piloted the *Tallahassee* through the eastern passage by night.

The run down the coast was uneventful, a few unimportant prizes being made. Many vessels were spoken, but most were foreign. A number were undoubtedly American, but to avoid capture had been registered abroad, and were sailing under other flags. I had intended going to Bermuda for another supply of coal, but the prevalence of yellow fever there prevented. As we approached Wilmington we were reminded, by sighting one or two steamers, that we were again in troubled waters. The first one we made out was a long, low, paddle-wheel boat, evidently a captured blockade-runner. By changing our course we soon parted company with her. Later in the day another was dodged. In running the blockade, if with good observation we were certain of our position, the best plan was to run direct for the Mound or harbor. If not, then better strike for the shore to the northward (if running for New Inlet), and follow it down. As the soundings are very regular, this could be easily done. The weather was hazy and smoky — so much so that we could not depend on our sights. I therefore ran in toward Masonboro Inlet, about thirty miles to the northward of Fort Fisher, making the land just at dark; then ran into five fathoms, and followed the shore, just outside the breakers curling up on the beach. A sharp lookout was kept, and the crew were at their quarters. The fires were freshened, and watched carefully to avoid smoking or flaming. The chief engineer had orders to get all he could out of her. I knew that one of the blockaders, if not more, would be found close to the shore; and soon one was made out ahead. I tried to pass inside, but found it impossible; the enemy's ship was almost in the surf. A vigilant officer certainly was in command. Our helm was put a-starboard, and we sheered out. At the same time the enemy signaled by flash-lights. I replied by burning a blue light. The signal was repeated by the first and by two others. I replied again by a false fire. Some valuable minutes were gained, but the enemy now appeared satisfied as to our character, and opened fire. We replied with all our battery, directing our guns by the flash of theirs. This was entirely unexpected, for they ceased firing, and began to signal again. Our reply was another broadside, to which they were not slow in responding. The *Tallahassee* was now heading the bar, going fourteen knots. Two or three others joined in the firing, and for some time it was very lively. But, like most night engagements, it was random firing. We were not struck, and the enemy were in more danger from their own fire than from mine.

Soon the Mound loomed up ahead, a welcome sight. Our signal-officer made our number to Fort Fisher, and it was answered. A few minutes later the range lights were set, and by their guidance we safely crossed the bar and anchored close under the fort. The next morning, at daybreak, the blockading fleet was seen lying about five miles off, all in a bunch, evidently discussing the events of the night. At sunrise we hoisted the Confederate flag at the fore, and saluted with twenty-one guns. The fort returned a like number. During the day we crossed the rip, and proceeded up the river to Wilmington. So ended an exciting and eventful cruise of a month. In this time we had made thirty-five captures, about half of which were square-rigged vessels.[224]

The *Tallahassee*, it is true, was built in England, but not for a blockade-runner. She was fitted out and equipped in a Confederate port. Of her armament, two guns were cast in Richmond, and one was captured. Her officers and crew were all in the service previous to joining her. She sailed from a Confederate port, and returned to one. She was regularly commissioned by the Navy Department, and was as legally a cruiser as was General Lee's force an army. Her status was entirely different from that of cruisers fitted out in England. The Geneva award was intended to cover only losses arising from the cruises of the *Alabama, Shenandoah*, etc., vessels fitted out or sailing from English ports, or which, like these, had never visited a Confederate port; and its recipients were at first wisely confined to those who could establish their losses from these vessels. But after paying all these, half of the £3,000,000 sterling still remained. After some years it was determined to divide it among the sufferers by all the cruisers. The claims presented to the court for the disposal of the award were of the most extraordinary character. I received from different attorneys letters asking for information upon points in regard to the *Tallahassee's* cruise, and inclosing schedules of losses of different parties. I have no idea how the court adjusted these losses; but I do know that if some of the claimants were paid ten per cent. of their demands, they were amply reimbursed for all losses. One captain of a small vessel put in a claim for $200 for a feather-bed, a hair-mattress, and a pair of blankets, and for nearly $800 worth of clothing! Another exhibit, of a mate, for losses called for $26 for a feather-bed. Another claimant had sixteen different suits of clothing, besides miscellaneous articles of wearing-apparel of all kinds—enough to furnish a Chatham-street shop. Nothing was left out: razor, brush, and cup, $3.50; shoe-brush and blacking, $1.03. Of course, every one, from the captain to the cook, had a watch and chain, generally gold, valued at from $100 to $250, never less. And these exhibits were all sworn to!

The *Tallahassee* made another short cruise, under Lieutenant Ward, and then returned to England. Later she was sold to the Japanese government as a cruiser.

Chapter 10

Escape of the Confederate Secretary of War

"Escape of the Confederate Secretary of War" was first published in the November 1893 issue of The Century Illustrated Monthly Magazine. *A slightly revised version of the piece, entitled "Escape of General Breckinridge," later appeared in the anthology* Famous Adventures and Prison Escapes of the Civil War *(1904). It is this latter text that is collected here. (The account was recently reprinted in two parts, under the title "Running by Land and Sea," in the December 2001 and the February 2002 issues of* Civil War Times Illustrated.*)*

The memoir, which is undoubtedly Wood's most exciting and colorful narrative, opens on 10 May 1865, the day that he and the other members of President Jefferson Davis' party of fleeing Confederates were captured by Union forces in Georgia. With considerable skill, Wood recounts his escape from captivity later that same day and his subsequent flight southward through Florida and then across the Straits of Florida to Cuba and exile. For most of this month-long, often harrowing adventure, Wood was joined by General John C. Breckinridge (the Confederacy's last secretary of war and a former vice president of the United States); Breckinridge's aide, Colonel James Wilson; Breckinridge's black servant, Thomas Ferguson; and two paroled soldiers, Sergeant Joseph J. O'Toole and Corporal Richard R. Russell.

The illustrations by the artist W. Taber that accompany the piece are taken from Century *magazine and are based on sketches provided by Wood.*

ESCAPE OF THE CONFEDERATE
SECRETARY OF WAR

As one of the aides of President Jefferson Davis, I left Richmond with him and his cabinet on April 2, 1865, the night of evacuation, and accompanied him through Virginia, the Carolinas, and Georgia, until his capture. Except Lieutenant Barnwell, I was the only one of the party who escaped. After our surprise, I was guarded by a trooper, a German, who had appropriated my horse and most of my belongings. I determined, if possible, to escape; but after witnessing Mr. Davis' unsuccessful attempt, I was doubtful of success. However, I consulted him, and he advised me to try. Taking my guard aside, I asked him, by signs (for he could speak little or no English), to accompany me outside the picket-line to the swamp, showing him at the same time a twenty-dollar gold piece. He took it, tried the weight of it in his hands, and put it between his teeth. Fully satisfied that it was not spurious, he escorted me with his carbine to the stream, the banks of which were lined with a few straggling alder-bushes and thick saw-grass. I motioned him to return to camp, only a few rods distant. He shook his head, saying, "*Nein, nein.*" I gave him another twenty-dollar gold piece; he chinked then together and held up two fingers. I turned my pockets inside out, and then, satisfied that I had no more, he left me.

Creeping a little farther into the swamp, I lay concealed for about three hours in the most painful position, sometimes moving a few yards almost *ventre à terre* to escape notice; for I was within hearing of the camps on each side of the stream, and often when the soldiers came down for water, or to water their horses, I was within a few yards of them. Some two hours or more passed thus before the party moved. The wagons left first, then the bugles sounded, and the president started on one of his carriage-horses, followed by his staff and a squadron of the enemy. Shortly after their departure I saw some one leading two abandoned horses into the swamp, and recognized Lieutenant Barnwell of our escort. Secreting the horses, we picked up from the debris of the camp parts of two saddles and bridles, and with some patching and tying fitted out our horses, as sad and war-worn animals as ever man bestrode. Though hungry and tired, we gave the remains of the camp provisions to a Mr. Fenn for dinner. He recommended us to Widow Paulk's, ten miles distant, an old lady rich in cattle alone.

The day after my escape, I met Judah P. Benjamin as M. Bonfals, a French gentleman traveling for information, in a light wagon, with Colonel Leovie, who acted as interpreter. With goggles on, his beard grown, a hat well over his face, and a large cloak hiding his figure, no one would have recognized him as the late secretary of state of the Confederacy. I told him of the capture of Mr. Davis and his party, and made an engagement to meet him near Madison, Florida, and there decide upon our future movements. He was anxious to push on, and left us to follow more leisurely, passing as paroled soldiers returning home. For the next three days we traveled as fast as our poor horses would permit, leading or driving them; for even if they had been strong enough, their backs were in such a condition that we could not ride. We held on to them simply in the hope that we might be able to dispose of them or exchange them to advantage; but we finally were forced to abandon one.

On the 13th we passed through Valdosta, the first place since leaving Washington, in upper Georgia, in which we were able to purchase anything. Here I secured two hickory shirts and a pair of socks, a most welcome addition to my outfit; for, except what I stood in, I had left all my baggage behind. Near Valdosta we found Mr. Osborne Barnwell, an uncle of my young friend, a refugee from the coast of South Carolina, where he had lost a beautiful estate, surrounded with all the comforts and elegances which wealth and a refined taste could offer. Here in the pine forests, as far as possible from the paths of war, and almost outside of civilization, he had brought his family of ladies and children, and with the aid of his servants, most of whom had followed him, had built with a few tools a rough log cabin with six or eight rooms, but without nails, screws, bolts, or glass— almost as primitive a building as Robinson Crusoe's. But, in spite of all drawbacks, the ingenuity and deft hands of the ladies had given to the premises an air of comfort and refinement that was most refreshing. Here I rested two days, enjoying the company of this charming family, with whom Lieutenant Barnwell remained. On the 15th I crossed into Florida, and rode to General Finegan's, near Madison. Here I met General Breckinridge, the late secretary of war of the Confederacy, alias Colonel Cabell, and his aide, Colonel Wilson — a pleasant encounter for both parties.

Mr. Benjamin had been in the neighborhood, but, hearing that the enemy were in Madison, had gone off at a tangent. We were fully posted as to the different routes to the seaboard by General Finegan, and discussed with him the most feasible way of leaving the country. I inclined to the eastern coast, and this was decided on. I exchanged my remaining horse with General Finegan for a better, giving him fifty dollars to boot. Leaving Madison, we crossed the Suwanee River at Moody's Ferry, and took the old St. Augustine road, but seldom traveled in late years, as it leads through a pine wilderness, and there is one stretch of twenty miles with only water of bad quality, at the Diable Sinks. I rode out of my way some fifteen miles to Mr. Yulee's, formerly senator of the United States, and afterward Confederate senator, hoping to meet Mr. Benjamin; but he was too wily to be found at the house of a friend. Mr. Yulee was absent on my arrival, but Mrs. Yulee, a charming lady, and one of a noted family of beautiful women, welcomed me heartily. Mr. Yulee returned during the night from Jacksonville, and gave me the first news of what was going on in the world that I had had for nearly a month, including the information that Mr. Davis and party had reached Hilton Head on their way north.

Another day's ride brought us to the house of the brothers William and Samuel Owens, two wealthy and hospitable gentlemen, near Orange Lake. Here I rejoined General Breckinridge, and we were advised to secure the services and experience of Captain Dickison. We sent to Waldo for him, and a most valuable friend he proved. During the war he had rendered notable services; among others he had surprised and captured the United States gunboat *Columbine* on the St. John's River, one of whose small boats he had retained, and kept concealed near the banks of the river. This boat with two of his best men he now put at our disposal, with orders to meet us on the upper St. John.

We now passed through a much more interesting country than the two or three hundred miles of pines we had just traversed. It was better watered, the forests were more diversified with varied species, occasionally thickets or hummocks were met with, and later these gave place to swamps and everglades with a tropical vegetation. The road led by Silver Spring, the clear and crystal waters of which show at the depth of hundreds of feet almost as distinctly as though seen through air.

We traveled incognito, known only to good friends, who sent us stage by stage from one to another, and by all we were welcomed most kindly. Besides those mentioned, I recall with gratitude the names of Judge Dawkins, Mr. Mann, Colonel Summers, Major Stork, all of whom overwhelmed us with kindness, offering us of everything they had. Of money they were as bare as ourselves, as Confederate currency had disappeared as suddenly as snow before a warm sun, and greenbacks were as yet unknown. Before leaving our friends, we laid in a three weeks' supply of stores; for we could not depend upon obtaining any further south.

On May 25 we struck the St. John's River at Fort Butler, opposite Volusia, where we met Russell and O'Toole, two of Dickison's command, in charge of the boat; and two most valuable and trustworthy companions they proved to be, either in camp or in the boat, as hunters or fishermen. The boat was a man-of-war's small four-oared gig; her outfit was scanty, but what was necessary we rapidly improvised. Here General Breckinridge and I gave our horses to our companions, and thus ended my long ride of a thousand miles from Virginia.

Stowing our supplies away, we bade good-by to our friends, and started up the river with a fair wind. Our party consisted of General Breckinridge; his aide, Colonel Wilson of Kentucky; the general's servant, Tom, who had been with him all through the war; besides Russell, O'Toole, and I — six in all. With our stores, arms, etc., it was a tight fit to get into the boat; there was no room to lie down or to stretch. At night we landed, and like old campaigners, were soon comfortable. But at midnight the rain came down in bucketfuls, and continued till nearly morning; and notwithstanding every effort, a large portion of our supplies were soaked and rendered worthless, and, what was worse, some of our powder shared the same fate.

Morning broke on a thoroughly drenched and unhappy company; but a little rum and water, with a corn-dodger and the rising sun, soon stirred us, and with a fair wind we made a good day's run — some thirty-five miles. Except the ruins of two huts, there was no sign that a human being had ever visited these waters, for the war and the occasional visit of a gunboat had driven off the few settlers. The river gradually became narrower and more tortuous as we approached its head waters. The banks are generally low, with a few sandy elevations, thickly wooded or swampy. Occasionally we passed a small opening, or savanna, on which were sometimes feeding a herd of wild cattle and deer; at the latter we had several potshots, all wide. Alligators, as immovable as the logs on which they rested, could be counted by hundreds, and of all sizes up to twelve or fifteen feet. Occasionally, as we passed uncomfortably near, we could not resist, even with our scant supply of ammunition, giving them a little cold lead between the head and shoulders, the only vulnerable place. With a fair wind we sailed the twelve miles across Lake Monroe, a pretty sheet of water, the deserted huts of Enterprise and Mellonville on each side. Above the lake the river became still narrower and more tortuous, dividing sometimes into numerous branches, most of which proved to be mere *culs-de-sac*. The long moss, reaching from the overhanging branches to the water, gave to the surroundings a most weird and funereal aspect.

On May 29 we reached Lake Harney, whence we determined to make the portage to Indian River. O'Toole was sent to look for some means of moving our boat. He returned next day with two small black bulls yoked to a pair of wheels such as are used by lumbermen. Their owner was a compound of Caucasian, African, and Indian, with the shrewdness of the white, the good temper of the negro, and the indolence of the red man. He was at first exorbitant in his demands; but a little money, some tobacco, and a spare fowling-piece made him happy, and he was ready to let us drive his beasts to the end of the peninsula. It required some skill to mount the boat securely on the wheels and to guard against any upsets or collisions, for our escape depended upon carrying it safely across.

The next morning we made an early start. Our course was an easterly one, through a roadless, flat, sandy pine-barren, with occasional thicket and swamp. From the word "go" trouble with the bulls began. Their owner seemed to think that in furnishing them he had fulfilled his part of the contract. They would neither "gee" or "haw"; if one started ahead, the other would go astern. If by accident they started ahead together, they would certainly bring up with their heads on each side of a tree. Occasionally they would lie down in a pool to get rid of the flies, and only by the most vigorous prodding could they be induced to move.

Paul, the owner, would loiter in the rear, but was always on hand when we halted for meals. Finally we told him, "No work, no grub; no drive bulls, no tobacco." This roused him to help us. Two days were thus occupied in covering eighteen miles. It would have been less labor to have tied the beasts, put them into the boat, and hauled it across the portage. The weather was intensely hot, and our time was made miserable by day with sand flies, and by night with mosquitoes.

The waters of Indian River were a most welcome sight, and we hoped that most of our troubles were over. Paul and his bulls of Bashan were gladly dismissed to the wilderness.[225] Our first care was to make good any defects in our boat: some leaks were stopped by a little calking and pitching. Already our supply of provisions began to give us anxiety: only bacon and sweet potatoes remained. The meal was wet and worthless, and, what was worse, all our salt had dissolved. However, with the waters alive with fish, and some game on shore, we hoped to pull through.

We reached Indian River, or lagoon, opposite Cape Canaveral. It extends along nearly the entire eastern coast of Florida, varying in width from three to six miles, and is separated from the Atlantic by a narrow sand ridge, which is pierced at different points by shifting inlets. It is very shoal, so much so that we were obliged to haul our boat out nearly half a mile before she would float, and the water is teeming with stingarees, sword-fish, crabs, etc. But once afloat, we headed to the southward with a fair wind.

For four days we continued to make good progress, taking advantage of every fair wind by night as well as by day. Here, as on the St. John's River, the same scene of desolation as far as human beings were concerned was presented. We passed a few deserted cabins, around which we were able to obtain a few cocoanuts and watermelons, a most welcome addition to our slim commissariat. Unfortunately, oranges were not in season. Whenever the breeze left us the heat was almost suffocating; there was no escape from it. If we landed, and sought any shade, the mosquitoes would drive us at once to the glare of the sun. When sleeping on shore, the best protection was to bury ourselves in the sand, with cap drawn down over the head (my buckskin gauntlets proved invaluable); if in the boat, to wrap the sail or tarpaulin around us. Besides this plague, sand-flies, gnats, swamp-flies, ants, and other insects abounded. The little black ant is especially bold and warlike. If, in making our beds in the sand, we disturbed one of their hives, they would rally in thousands to the attack, and the only safety was in a hasty shake and change of residence.

Passing Indian River inlet, the river broadens, and there is a thirty-mile straight-away course to Gilbert's Bar, or Old Inlet, now closed; then begin the Juniper Narrows, where the channel is crooked, narrow, and often almost closed by the dense growth of mangroves, juniper, saw-grass, etc., making a jungle that only a water-snake could penetrate. Several times we lost our reckoning, and had to retreat and take a fresh start; an entire day was lost in these everglades, which extend across the entire peninsula. Finally, by good luck, we stumbled on a short "haulover" to the sea, and determined at once to take advantage of it, and to run our boat across and launch her in the Atlantic. A short half-mile over the sand-dunes, and we were clear of the swamps and marshes of Indian River, and were reveling in the Atlantic, free, at least for a time, from mosquitoes, which had punctured and bled us for the last three weeks.

"Sand as a defense against mosquitos" (*The Century Illustrated Monthly Magazine*, November 1893).

On Sunday, June 4, we passed Jupiter Inlet, with nothing in sight. The lighthouse had been destroyed the first year of the war. From this point we had determined to cross Florida Channel to the Bahamas, about eighty miles; but the wind was ahead, and we could do nothing but work slowly to the southward, waiting for a slant. It was of course a desperate venture to cross this distance in a small open boat, which even a moderate sea would swamp. Our provisions now became a very serious question. As I have said, we had lost all the meal, and the sweet potatoes, our next main-stay, were sufficient only for two days more. We had but little more ammunition than was necessary for our revolvers, and these we might be called upon to use at any time.

Very fortunately for us, it was the time of the year when the green turtle deposits its eggs. Russell and O'Toole were old beach-combers, and had hunted eggs before. Sharpening a stick, they pressed it into the sand as they walked along, and wherever it entered easily they would dig. After some hours' search we were successful in finding a nest which had not been destroyed, and I do not think prospectors were ever more gladdened by the sight of "the yellow" than we were at our find. The green turtle's egg is about the size of a walnut, with a white skin like parchment that you can tear, but not break. The yolk will cook hard, but the longer you boil the egg the softer the white becomes. The flavor is not unpleasant, and for the first two days we enjoyed them; but then we were glad to vary the fare with a few shell-fish and even with snails.

From Cape Canaveral to Cape Florida the coast trends nearly north and south in a straight line, so that we could see at a long distance anything going up or down the shore. Some distance to the southward of Jupiter Inlet we saw a steamer coming down, running close to the beach to avoid the three- and four-knot current of the stream. From her yards and general appearance I soon made her out to be a cruiser, so we hauled our boat well up on the sands, turned it over on its side, and went back among the palmettos. When abreast of us and not more than a half-mile off, with colors flying, we could see the officer of the deck and others closely scanning the shore. We were in hope they would look upon our boat as flotsam and jetsam, of which there was more or less strewn upon the beach. To our great relief, the cruiser passed us, and when she was two miles or more to the southward we ventured out and approached the boat, but the sharp lookout saw us, and, to our astonishment, the steamer came swinging about, and headed up the coast. The question at once arose, What was the best course to pursue? The general thought we had better take to the bush again, and leave the boat, hoping they would not disturb it. Colonel Wilson agreed with his chief. I told him that since we had been seen, the enemy would certainly destroy or carry off the boat, and the loss meant, if not starvation, at least privation, and no hope of escaping from the country. Besides, the mosquitoes would suck us as dry as Egyptian mummies.

I proposed that we should meet them half-way, in company with Russell and O'Toole, who were paroled men, and fortunately had their papers with them, and I offered to row off and see what was wanted. He agreed, and, launching our boat and throwing in two buckets of eggs, we pulled out. By this time the steamer was abreast of us, and had lowered a boat, which met us half-way. I had one oar, and O'Toole the other. To the usual hail I paid no attention except to stop rowing. A ten-oared cutter with a smart-looking crew dashed alongside. The sheen was not yet off the lace and buttons of the youngster in charge. With revolver in hand he asked us who we were, where we came from, and where we were going. "Cap'n," said I, "please put away that-ar pistol—I don't like the looks of it—and I'll tell you all about us. We've been rebs, and there ain't no use saying we weren't; but it's all up now, and we got home too late to put in a crop, so we just made up our minds to come down shore and see if we couldn't find something. It's all right, Cap'n; we've got our papers. Want to see 'em? Got 'em fixed up at Jacksonville." O'Toole and Russell handed him their paroles, which he said were all right. He asked for mine. I turned my pockets out, looked in my hat, and said: "I must er dropped mine in camp, but 't is just the same as theirn." He asked who was ashore. I told him, "There's more of we-uns b'iling some turtle-eggs for dinner. Cap'n, I'd like to swap some eggs for tobacco or bread." His crew soon produced from the slack of their frocks pieces of plug, which they passed on board in exchange for our eggs. I told the youngster if he'd come to camp we'd give him as many as he could eat. Our hospitality was declined.

Among other questions he asked if there were any batteries on shore — a battery on a beach where there was not a white man within a hundred miles! "Up oars—let go forward—let fall—give 'way!" were all familiar orders; but never before had they sounded so welcome. As they shoved off, the coxswain said to the youngster, "That looks like a man-of-war's gig, sir"; but he paid no attention to him. We pulled leisurely ashore, watching the cruiser. The boat went up to the davits at a run, and she started to the southward again. The general was very much relieved, for it was a narrow escape.

The wind still holding to the southward and eastward, we could work only slowly to the southward, against wind and current. At times we suffered greatly for want of water; our usual resource was to dig for it, but often it was so brackish and warm that when extreme thirst forced its use the consequences were violent pains and retchings. One morning we saw a few wigwams ashore, and pulled in at once and landed. It was a party of Seminoles who had come out of the everglades like the bears to gather eggs. They received us kindly, and we devoured ravenously the remnants of their breakfast of fish and *kountee*. Only the old chief spoke a little English. Not more than two or three hundred of this once powerful and warlike tribe remain in Florida; they occupy some islands in this endless swamp to the southward of Lake Okeechobee. They have but little intercourse with the whites, and come out on the coast only at certain seasons to fish.

We were very anxious to obtain some provisions from them, but excepting *kountee* they had nothing to spare. This is an esculent resembling arrowroot, which they dig, pulverize, and use as flour. Cooked in the ashes, it makes a palatable but tough cake, which we enjoyed after our long abstinence from bread. The old chief took advantage of our eagerness for supplies, and determined to replenish his powder-horn. Nothing else would do; not even an old coat, or fish-hooks, or a cavalry saber would tempt him. Powder only he would have for their long, heavy small-bore rifles with flint-locks, such as Davy Crockett used. We reluctantly divided with him our very scant supply in exchange for some of their flour. We parted good friends, after smoking the pipe of peace.

On the 7th, off New River inlet, we discovered a small sail standing to the northward. The breeze was very light, so we downed our sail, got out oars, and gave chase. The stranger stood out to seaward, and endeavored to escape; but slowly we overhauled her, and finally a shot caused her mainsail to drop. As we pulled alongside I saw from the dress of the crew of three that they were man-of-war's men, and divined that they were deserters. They were thoroughly frightened at first, for our appearance was not calculated to impress them favorably. To our questions they returned evasive answers or were silent, and finally asked by what authority we had overhauled them. We told them that the war was not over so far as we were concerned; that they were our prisoners, and their boat our prize; that they were both deserters and pirates, the punishment of which was death; but that under the circumstances we would not surrender them to the first cruiser we met, but would take their paroles and exchange boats. To this they strenuously objected.

They were well armed, and although we outnumbered them five to three (not counting Tom), still, if they could get the first bead on us the chances were about equal. They were desperate, and not disposed to surrender their boat without a tussle. The general and I stepped into their boat, and ordered the spokesman and leader to go forward. He hesitated a moment, and two revolvers looked him in the face. Sullenly he obeyed our orders. The general said, "Wilson, disarm that man." The colonel, with pistol in hand, told him to hold up his hands. He did so while the colonel drew from his belt a navy revolver and a sheath-knife. The other two made no further show of resistance, but handed us their arms. The crew disposed of, I made an examination of our capture. Unfortunately, her supply of provisions was very small — only some "salt-horse" and hard-tack, with a breaker of fresh water, and we exchanged part of them for some of our *kountee* and turtles' eggs. But it was in our new boat that we were particularly fortunate: sloop-rigged, not much longer than our gig, but with more beam and plenty of free-board, decked over to the mast, and well found in sails and rigging. After our experience in a boat the gun-wale of which was not more than eighteen inches out of the water, we felt that we had a craft able to cross the Atlantic. Our prisoners, submitting to the inevitable, soon made themselves at home in their new boat, became more communicative, and wanted some information as to the best course by which to reach Jacksonville or Savannah. We were glad to give them the benefit of our experience and on parting handed them their knives and two revolvers, for which they were very thankful.

Later we were abreast of Green Turtle Key, with wind light and ahead; still, with all these drawbacks, we were able to make some progress. Our new craft worked and sailed well, after a little addition of ballast. Before leaving the coast, we found it would be necessary to call at Fort Dallas or some other point for supplies. It was running a great risk, for we did not know whom we should find there, whether friend or foe. But without at least four or five days' rations of some kind, it would not be safe to attempt the passage across the Gulf Stream. However, before venturing to do so, we determined to try to replenish our larder with eggs. Landing on the beach, we hunted industriously for some hours, literally scratching for a living; but the ground had evidently been most effectually gone over before, as the tracks of bears proved. A few onions, washed from some passing vessel, were eagerly devoured. We scanned the washings along the strand in vain for anything that would satisfy hunger. Nothing remained but to make the venture of stopping at the fort.

This fort, like many others, was established during the Seminole war, and at its close was abandoned. It is near the mouth of the Miami River, a small stream which serves as an outlet to the overflow of the everglades. Its banks are crowded to the water's edge with tropical verdure, with many flowering plants and creepers, all the colors of which are reflected in its clear waters. The old barracks were in sight as we slowly worked our way against the current. Located in a small clearing, with cocoanut-trees in the foreground, the white buildings made, with a

"Searching for turtles' eggs" (*The Century Illlustrated Monthly Magazine*, November 1893).

backing of deep green, a very pretty picture. We approached cautiously, not knowing with what reception we should meet. As we neared the small wharf, we found waiting some twenty or thirty men, of all colors, from the pale Yankee to the ebony Congo, all armed; a more motley and villainous-looking crew never trod the deck of one of Captain Kidd's ships. We saw at once with whom we had to deal — deserters from the army and navy of both sides, with a mixture of Spaniards and Cubans, outlaws and renegades.

A burly villain, towering head and shoulders above his companions, and whose shaggy black head scorned any covering, hailed us in broken English, and asked who we were. Wreckers, I replied; that we had left our vessel outside, and had come in for water and provisions. He asked where we had left our vessel, and her name, evidently suspicious, which was not surprising, for our appearance was certainly against us. Our head-gear was unique: the general wore a straw hat that flapped over his head like the ears of an elephant; Colonel Wilson, an old cavalry cap that had lost its visor; another, a turban made of some number 4 duck canvas; and all were in our shirt-sleeves, the color of which were as varied as Joseph's coat. I told him we had left her to the northward a few miles, that a gun-boat had spoken us a few hours before, and had overhauled our papers, and had found them all right. After a noisy powwow we were told to land, that our papers might be examined. I said no, but if a canoe were sent off,

I would let one of our men go on shore and buy what we wanted. I was determined not to trust our boat within a hundred yards of the shore.

Finally a canoe paddled by two negroes came off, and said no one but the captain would be permitted to land. O'Toole volunteered to go, but the boatmen would not take him, evidently having had their orders. I told them to tell their chief that we had intended to spend a few pieces of gold with them, but since he would not permit it, we would go elsewhere for supplies. We got out our sweeps, and moved slowly down the river, a light breeze helping us. The canoe returned to the shore, and soon some fifteen or twenty men crowded into four or five canoes and dugouts, and started for us. We prepared for action, determined to give them a warm reception. Even Tom looked after his carbine, putting on a fresh cap.

Though outnumbered three to one, still we were well under cover in our boat, and could rake each canoe as it came up. We determined to take all the chances, and to open fire as soon as they came within range. I told Russell to try a shot at one some distance ahead of the others. He broke two paddles on one side and hit one man, not a bad beginning. This canoe dropped to the rear at once; the occupant of the others opened fire, but their shooting was wild from the motions of their small crafts. The general tried and missed; Tom thought he could do better than his master, and made a good line shot, but short. The general advised husbanding our ammunition until they came within easy range. Waiting a little while, Russell and the colonel fired together, and the bowman in the nearest canoe rolled over, nearly upsetting her. They were now evidently convinced that

"Exchanging the boat for the sloop" (*The Century Illustrated Monthly Magazine*, November 1893).

we were in earnest, and, after giving us an ineffectual volley, paddled together to hold a council of war. Soon a single canoe with three men started for us with a white flag. We hove to, and waited for them to approach. When within hail, I asked what was wanted. A white man, standing in the stern, with two negroes paddling, replied:

"What did you fire on us for? We are friends."

"Friends do not give chase to friends."

"We wanted to find out who you are."

"I told you who we are; and if you are friends, sell us some provisions."

"Come on shore, and you can get what you want."

Our wants were urgent, and it was necessary, if possible, to make some terms with them; but it would not be safe to venture near their lair again. We told them that if they would bring us some supplies we would wait, and pay them well in gold. The promise of gold served as a bait to secure some concession. After some parleying it was agreed that O'Toole should go on shore in their canoe, be allowed to purchase some provisions, and return in two hours. The buccaneer thought the time too short, but I insisted that if O'Toole were not brought back in two hours, I would speak the first gunboat I met, and return with her and have their nest of freebooters broken up. Time was important, for we had noticed soon after we

"Through a shallow lagoon" (*The Century Illustrated Monthly Magazine*, November 1893).

had started down the river a black column of smoke ascending from near the fort, undoubtedly a signal to some of their craft in the vicinity to return, for I felt convinced that they had other craft besides canoes at their disposal; hence their anxiety to detain us. O'Toole was told to be as dumb as an oyster as to ourselves, but wide awake as to the designs of our dubious friends. The general gave him five eagles for his purchase, tribute-money. He jumped into the canoe, and all returned to the fort. We dropped anchor underfoot to await his return, keeping a sharp lookout for any strange sail.

The two hours passed in pleasant surmises as to what he would bring off; another half-hour passed, and no sign of his return; and we began to despair of our anticipated feast, and of O'Toole, a bright young Irishman, whose good qualities had endeared him to us all. The anchor was up, and slowly with a light breeze we drew away from the river, debating what should be our next move. The fort was shut in by a projecting point, and three or four miles had passed when the welcome sight of a canoe astern made us heave to. It was O'Toole with two negroes, a bag of hard bread, two hams, some rusty salt pork, sweet potatoes, fruit, and, most important of all, two breakers of water and a keg of New England rum. While O'Toole gave us his experience, a ham was cut, and a slice between two of hardtack, washed down with a jorum of rum and water, with a dessert of oranges and bananas, was a feast to us more enjoyable than any ever eaten at Delmonico's or the Café Riche.

On his arrival on shore, our ambassador had been taken to the quarters of Major Valdez, who claimed to be an officer of the Federals, and by him he was thoroughly cross-examined. He had heard of the breaking up of the Confederacy, but not of the capture of Mr. Davis, and was evidently skeptical of our story as to being wreckers, and connected us in some way with the losing party, either as persons of note or a party escaping with treasure. However, O'Toole baffled all his queries, and was proof against both blandishments and threats. He learned what he had expected, that they were looking for the return of a schooner; hence the smoke signal, and the anxiety to detain us as long as possible. It was only when he saw us leaving, after waiting over two hours, that the major permitted him to make a few purchases and rejoin us.

Night, coming on, found us inside of Key Biscayne, the beginning of the system of innumerable keys, or small islands, extending from this point to the Tortugas, nearly two hundred miles east and west, at the extremity of the peninsula. Of coral formation, as soon as it is built up to the surface of the water it crumbles under the action of the sea and sun. Sea-fowl rest upon it, dropping the seed of some marine plants, or the hard mangrove is washed ashore on it, and its all-embracing roots soon spread in every direction; so are formed these keys. Darkness and shoal water warned us to anchor. We passed an unhappy night fighting mosquitoes. As the sun rose, we saw to the eastward a schooner of thirty or forty tons standing down toward us with a light wind; no doubt it was one from the fort sent in pursuit. Up anchor, up sail, out sweeps, and we headed down Biscayne Bay, a shoal sheet of water between the reefs and mainland. The wind rose with the sun, and, being to windward, the schooner had the benefit of it first, and was fast overhauling us.

The water was shoaling, which I was not sorry to see, for our draft must have been from two to three feet less than that of our pursuer, and we recognized that our best chance of escape was by drawing him into shoal water, while keeping afloat ourselves. By the color and break of the water I saw that we were approaching a part of the bay where the shoals appeared to extend nearly across, with narrow channels between them like the furrows in a plowed field, with occasional openings from one channel into another. Some of the shoals were just awash, others bare. Ahead was a reef on which there appeared but very little water. I could see no opening into the channel beyond. To attempt to haul by the wind on either tack would bring us in a few minutes under fire of the schooner now coming up hand over hand. I ordered the ballast to be thrown overboard, and determined, as our only chance, to attempt to force her over the reef. She was headed for what looked like a little breakwater on our port bow. As

"Over a coral-reef" (*The Century Illustrated Monthly Magazine*, November 1893).

the ballast went overboard we watched the bottom anxiously; the water shoaled rapidly, and the grating of the keel over the coral, with that peculiar tremor most unpleasant to a seaman under any circumstances, told us our danger. As the last of the ballast went overboard she forged ahead, and then brought up. Together we went overboard, and sank to our waists in the black, pasty mud, through which at intervals branches of rotten coral projected, which only served to make the bottom more treacherous and difficult to work on. Relieved of a half-ton of our weight, our sloop forged ahead three or four lengths, and then brought up again. We pushed her forward some distance, but as the water lessened, notwithstanding our efforts, she stopped.

Looking astern, we saw the schooner coming up wing and wing, not more than a mile distant. Certainly the prospect was blue; but one chance was left, to sacrifice everything in the boat. Without hesitation, overboard went the provisions except a few biscuits; the oars were made fast to the main-sheet alongside, and a breaker of water, the anchor and chain, all spare rope, indeed everything that weighed a pound, was dropped alongside, and then, three on each side, our shoulders under the boat's bilges, at the word we lifted together, and foot by foot moved her forward. Sometimes the water would deepen a little and relieve us; again it would shoal. Between the coral-branches we would sink at times to our necks in the slime and water, our limbs lacerated with the sharp projecting points. Fortunately, the wind helped us; keeping all sail on, thus for more than a hundred yards we toiled, until the water deepened and the reef was passed. Wet, foul, bleeding, with hardly strength enough to climb into the boat, we were safe at last for a time. As we cleared the shoal, the schooner hauled by the wind, and opened fire from a nine- or twelve-pounder; but we were at long range, and the firing was wild. With a fair wind we soon opened the distance between us.

General Breckinridge, thoroughly used up, threw himself down in the bottom of the boat; at which Tom, always on the lookout for his master's comfort, said, "Marse John, s'pose you take a little rum and water." This proposal stirred us all. The general rose, saying, "Yes, indeed, Tom, I will; but where is the rum?" supposing it had been sacrificed with everything else.

"I sees you pitchin' eberyt'ing away; I jes put this jug in hyar, 'ca'se I 'lowed you'd want some."

Opening a locker in the transom, he took out the jug. Never was a potion more grateful; we were faint and thirsty, and it acted like a charm, and, bringing up on another reef, we were ready for another tussle. Fortunately, this proved only a short lift. In the mean time the schooner had passed through the first reef by an opening, as her skipper was undoubtedly familiar with these waters. Still another shoal was ahead; instead of again lifting our sloop over it, I hauled by the wind, and stood for what looked like an opening to the eastward. Our pursuers were on the opposite tack and fast approaching; a reef intervened, and when abeam, distant about half a mile, they opened fire both with their small arms and boat-gun. The second shot from the latter was well directed; it grazed our mast and carried away the luff of the mainsail. Several Minié balls struck on our sides without penetrating; we did not reply, and kept under cover. When abreast of a break in the reef, we up helm, and again went off before the wind. The schooner was now satisfied that she could not overhaul us, and stood off to the northward.

Free from our enemy, we were now able to take stock of our supplies and determine what to do. Our provisions consisted of about ten pounds of hard bread, a twenty-gallon breaker of water, two thirds full, and three gallons of rum. Really a fatality appeared to follow us as regards our commissariat. Beginning with our first drenching on the St. John's, every successive supply had been lost, and now what we had bought with so much trouble yesterday, the sellers compelled us to sacrifice to-day. But our first care was to ballast the sloop, for without it she was so crank as to be unseaworthy. This was not an easy task; the shore of all the keys, as well as that of the mainland in sight, was low and swampy, and covered to the water's edge with a dense growth of mangroves. What made matters worse, we were without any ground-tackle.

At night we were up to Elliott's Key, and anchored by making fast to a sweep shoved into the muddy bottom like a shad-pole. When the wind went down, the mosquitoes came off in clouds. We wrapped ourselves in the sails from head to feet, with only our nostrils exposed. At daylight we started again to the westward, looking for a dry spot where we might land, get ballast, and possibly some supplies. A few palm-trees rising from the mangroves indicated a spot where we might find a little *terra firma*. Going in as near as was prudent, we waded ashore, and found a small patch of sand and coral elevated a few feet above the everlasting swamp. Some six or eight cocoa-palms rose to the height of forty or fifty feet, and under their umbrella-like tops we could see the bunches of green fruit. It was a question how to get at it. Without saying a word, Tom went on board the boat, brought off a piece of canvas, cut a strip a yard long, tied the ends together, and made two holes for his big toes. The canvas, stretched between his feet, embraced the rough bark so that he rapidly ascended. He threw down the green nuts, and, cutting through the thick shell, we found about half a pint of milk. The general suggested a little milk-punch. All the trees were stripped, and what we did not use we saved for sea-stores.

To ballast our sloop was our next care. The jib was unbent, the sheet and head were brought together and made into a sack. This was filled with sand, and, slung on an oar, was shouldered by two and carried on board.

Leaving us so engaged, the general started to try to knock over some of the numerous water-fowl in sight. He returned in an hour thoroughly used up from his struggles in the swamp, but with two pelicans and a white crane. In the stomach of one of the first were a dozen or more mullet from six to nine inches in length, which had evidently just been swallowed. We cleaned them, and wrapping them in palmetto-leaves, roasted them in the ashes, and they proved delicious. Tom took the birds in hand, and as he was an old campaigner, who had cooked everything from a stalled ox to a crow, we had faith in his ability to make them palatable. He tried to pick them, but soon abandoned it, and skinned them. We looked on anxiously, ready after our first course of fish for something more substantial. He broiled them, and with a flourish laid one before the general on a clean leaf, saying, "I 's 'feared, Marse John, it's tough as an old muscovy drake."

"Let me try it, Tom."

After some exertion he cut off a mouthful, while we anxiously awaited the verdict. Without a word he rose and disappeared into the bushes. Returning in a few minutes, he told Tom to remove the game. His tone and expression satisfied us that pelican would not keep us from starving. The colonel thought the crane might be better, but a taste satisfied us that it was no improvement.

Hungry and tired, it was nearly night before we were ready to move; and, warned by our sanguinary experience of the previous night, we determined to haul off from the shore as far as possible, and get outside the range of the mosquitoes. It was now necessary to determine upon our future course. We had abandoned all hope of reaching the Bahamas, and the nearest foreign shore was that of Cuba, distant across the Gulf Stream from our present position about two hundred miles, or three or four days' sail, with the winds we might expect at this season. With the strictest economy our provisions would not last so long. However, nearly a month in the swamps and among the keys of Florida, in the month of June, had prepared us to face almost any risk to escape from those shores, and it was determined to start in the morning for Cuba.

Well out in the bay we hove to, and passed a fairly comfortable night; next day we started for Caesar's Canal, a passage between Elliott's Key and Key Largo. The channel was crooked and puzzling, leading through a labyrinth of mangrove islets, around which the current of the Gulf Stream was running like a sluice; we repeatedly got aground, when we would jump overboard and push off. So we worked all day before we

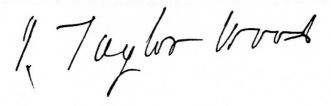

Wood's signature.

were clear of the keys and outside among the reefs, which extend three or four miles beyond. Waiting again for daylight, we threaded our way through them, and with a light breeze from the eastward steered south, thankful to feel again the pulsating motion of the ocean.

Several sail and one steamer were in sight during the day, but all at a distance. Constant exposure had tanned us the color of mahogany, and our legs and feet were swollen and blistered from being so much in salt water, and the action of the hot sun on them made them excessively painful. Fortunately, but little exertion was now necessary, and our only relief was in lying still, with an impromptu awning over us. General Breckinridge took charge of the water and rum, doling it out at regular intervals, a tot at a time, determined to make it last as long as possible.

Toward evening the wind was hardly strong enough to enable us to hold our own against the stream. At ten, Carysfort Light was abeam, and soon after a dark bank of clouds rising in the eastern sky betokened a change of wind and weather. Everything was made snug and lashed securely, with two reefs in the mainsail, and the bonnet taken off the jib. I knew from experience what we might expect from summer squalls in the straits of Florida. I took the helm, the general the sheet, Colonel Wilson was stationed by the halyards, Russell and O'Toole were prepared to bail. Tom, thoroughly demoralized, was already sitting in the bottom of the boat, between the general's knees. The sky was soon completely overcast with dark, lowering clouds; the darkness, which could almost be felt, was broken every few minutes by lurid streaks of lightning chasing one another through black abysses. Fitful gusts of wind were the heralds of the coming blast. Great drops of rain fell like the scattering fire of a skirmish-line, and with a roar like a thousand trumpets we heard the blast coming, giving us time only to lower everything and get the stern of the boat to it, for our only chance was to run with the storm until the rough edge was taken off, and then heave to. I cried, "All hands down!" as the gale struck us with

"A rough night in the Gulf Stream" (*The Century Illustrated Monthly Magazine*, November 1893).

the force of a thunderbolt, carrying a wall of white water with it which burst over us like a cataract.

I thought we were swamped as I clung desperately to the tiller, though thrown violently against the boom. But after the shock, our brave little boat, though half filled, rose and shook herself like a spaniel. The mast bent like a whip-stick, and I expected to see it blown out of her, but, gathering way, we flew with the wind. The surface was lashed into foam as white as the driven snow. The lightning and artillery of the heavens were incessant, blinding, and deafening; involuntarily we bowed our heads, utterly helpless. Soon the heavens were opened, and the floods came down like a waterspout. I knew then that the worst of it had passed, and though one fierce squall succeeded another, each one was tamer. The deluge, too, helped to beat down the sea. To give an order was impossible, for I could not be heard; I could only, during the flashes, make signs to Russell and O'Toole to bail. Tying themselves and their buckets to the thwarts, they went to work and soon relieved her of a heavy load.

From the general direction of the wind I knew without compass or any other guide that we were running to the westward, and, I feared, were gradually approaching the dreaded reefs, where in such a sea our boat would have been reduced to match-wood in a little while. Therefore, without waiting for the wind or sea to moderate, I determined to heave to, hazardous as it was to attempt anything of the kind. Giving the colonel the helm, I lashed the end of the gaff to the boom, and then loosed enough of the mainsail to goose-wing it, or make a leg-of-mutton sail of it. Then watching for a lull or a smooth time, I told him to put the helm a-starboard and let her come to on the port tack, head to the southward, and at the same time I hoisted the sail. She came by the wind quickly without shipping a drop of water, but as I was securing the halyards the colonel gave her too much helm, bringing the wind on the other bow, the boom flew round and knocked my feet from under me, and overboard I went. Fortunately, her way was deadened, and as I came up I seized the sheet, and with the general's assistance scrambled on board. For twelve hours or more I did not trust the helm to any one.

The storm passed over to the westward with many a departing growl and threat. But the wind still blew hoarsely from the eastward with frequent gusts against the stream, making a heavy, sharp sea. In the trough of it the boat was becalmed, but as she rose on the crest of the waves even the little sail set was as much as she could stand up under, and she had to be nursed carefully; for if she had fallen off, one breaker would have swamped us, or any accident to sail or spar would have been fatal: but like a gull on the waters, our brave little craft rose and breasted every billow.

By noon the next day the weather had moderated sufficiently to make more sail, and the sea went down at the same time. Then, hungry and thirsty, Tom was thought of. During the gale he had remained in the bottom of the boat as motionless as a log. As he was roused up, he asked:

"Marse John, whar is you, and whar is you goin'? 'Fore de Lord, I never want to see a boat again."

"Come, Tom, get us something to drink, and see if there is anything left to eat," said the general. But Tom was helpless.

The general served out a small ration of water and rum, every drop of which was precious. Our small store of bread was found soaked, but, laid in the sun, it partly dried, and was, if not palatable, at least a relief to hungry men.

During the next two days the weather was moderate, and we stood to the southward; several sail were in sight, but at a distance. We were anxious to speak one even at some risk, for our supplies were down to a pint of rum in water each day under a tropical sun, with two water-soaked biscuits. On the afternoon of the second day a brig drifted slowly down toward us; we made signals that we wished to speak her, and, getting out our sweeps, pulled for her. As we neared her, the captain hailed and ordered us to keep off. I replied that we were shipwrecked men, and only wanted some provisions. As we rounded to under his stern, we could see that he had all his crew of seven or eight men at quarters. He stood on the taffrail with a revolver in hand, his two mates with muskets, the cook with a huge tormentor, and the crew with handspikes.

"I tell you again, keep off, or I'll let fly."

"Captain, we won't go on board if you will give us some provisions; we are starving."

"Keep off, I tell you. Boys, make ready."

One of the mates drew a bead on me; our eyes met in a line over the sights on the barrel. I help up my right hand.

"Will you fire on an unarmed man? Captain, you are no sailor, or you would not refuse to help shipwrecked men."

"How do I know who you are? And I've got no grub to spare."

"Here is a passenger who is able to pay you," said I, pointing to the general.

"Yes, I will pay you for anything you let us have."

The captain now held a consultation with his officers, and then said: "I'll give you some water and bread. I've got nothing else. But you must not come alongside."

A small keg, or breaker, was thrown overboard and picked up, with a bag of fifteen or twenty pounds of hardtack. This was the reception given us by the brig *Neptune* of Bangor. But when the time and place are considered, we cannot wonder at the captain's precautions, for a more piratical-looking party than we never sailed the Spanish main. General Breckinridge, bronzed the color of mahogany, unshaven, with long mustache, wearing a blue flannel shirt open at the neck, exposing his broad chest, with an old slouch hat, was a typical buccaneer. Thankful for what we had received, we parted company. Doubtless the captain reported on his arrival home a blood-curdling story of his encounter with pirates off the coast of Cuba.

"Marse John, I thought the war was done. Why didn't you tell dem folks who you was?" queried Tom. The general told Tom they were Yankees, and would not believe us. "Is dar any Yankees whar you going?— 'ca'se if dar is, we best go back to old Kentucky." He was made easy on this point, and, with an increase in our larder, became quite perky. A change in the color of the water showed us that we were on soundings, and had crossed the Stream, and soon after we came in sight of some rocky islets, which I recognized as Double-Headed Shot Keys, thus fixing our position; for our chart, with the rest of our belongings, had disappeared, or had been destroyed by water, as the heavens, by day and night, were our only guide, our navigation was necessarily very uncertain. For the next thirty miles our course to the southward took us over Salt Key Bank, where the soundings varied from three to five fathoms, but so clear was the water that it was hard to believe that the coral, the shells, and the marine flowers were not within arm's reach. Fishes of all sizes and colors darted by us in every direction. The bottom of the bank was a constantly varying kaleidoscope of beauty. But to starving men, with not a mouthful in our grasp, the display of food was tantalizing. Russell, who was an expert swimmer, volunteered to dive for some conchs and shell-fish; oysters there were none. Asking us to keep a sharp lookout on the surface of the water for sharks, which generally swim with the dorsal fin exposed, he went down and brought up a couple of live conchs about the size of a man's fist. Breaking the shell, we drew the quivering body out. Without its coat it looked like a huge grub, and not more inviting. The general asked Tom to try it.

"Glory, Marse John, I'm mighty hungry, nebber so hungry sense we been in de almy, and I'm just ready for old mule, pole-cat, or any'ting 'cept dis worm."

After repeated efforts to dissect it we agreed with Tom, and found it no more edible than a pickled football. However, Russell, diving again, brought up bivalves with a very thin shell and beautiful colors, in shape like a large pea-pod. These we found tolerable; they served to satisfy in some small degree our craving for food. The only drawback was that eating them produced great thirst, which is much more difficult to bear than hunger. We found partial relief in keeping our heads and bodies wet with salt water.

On the sixth day from the Florida coast we crossed Nicholas Channel with fair wind. Soon after we made the Cuban coast, and stood to the westward, hoping to sight something which would determine our position. After a run of some hours just outside of the coral-reefs, we sighted in the distance some vessels at anchor. As we approached, a large town was visible at the head of the bay, which proved to be Cardenas. We offered prayful thanks for our wonderful escape, and anchored just off the custom-house, and waited some time for the health officer to give us pratique. But as no one came off in answer to our signals, I went on shore to report at the custom-house. It was some time before I could make them comprehend that we were from Florida, and anxious to land. Their astonishment was great at the size of our boat, and they could hardly believe we had crossed in it. Our arrival produced as much sensation as would that of a liner. We might have been filibusters in disguise. The governor-general had to be telegraphed to; numerous papers were made out and signed; a register was made out for the sloop *No Name*; then we had to make a visit to the governor before we were allowed to go to a hotel to get something to eat. After a cup of coffee and a light meal I had a warm bath, and donned some clean linen which our friends provided.

We were overwhelmed with attentions, and when the governor-general telegraphed that General Breckinridge was to be treated as one holding his position and rank, the officials became as obsequious as they had been overbearing and suspicious. The next day one of the governor-general's aides-de-camp arrived from Havana, with an invitation for the general and the party to visit him, which we accepted, and after two days' rest took the train for the capital. A special car was placed at our disposal, and on our arrival the general was received with all the honors. We were driven to the palace, had a long interview, and dined with Governor-General Concha. The transition from a small open boat at sea, naked and starving, to the luxuries and comforts of civilized life was as sudden as it was welcome and thoroughly appreciated.

At Havana our party separated. General Breckinridge and Colonel Wilson have since crossed the great river; Russell and O'Toole returned to Florida. I should be glad to know what has become of faithful Tom.

Appendix 1

The Capture of
the USS *Underwriter*

As previously noted, not all of John Taylor Wood's Civil War experiences were recorded in his published memoirs. It is particularly regrettable that he did not leave an account of his distinguished service as a raider in Virginia and Carolina waters at various times during the 1862–1864 period.

One of his boldest expeditions was the capture of the gunship USS Underwriter *on the Neuse River near New Bern, North Carolina, in 1864.[226] In the absence of Wood's own memoir of this event, it is fortunate that J. Thomas Scharf, who served under Wood during the raid, provided a full description of the action in his monumental* History of the Confederate States Navy from Its Organization to the Surrender of its Last Vessel *(1887). Since it is known that Wood provided some assistance to Scharf in the writing of the* History of the Confederate States Navy, *it is possible that the account which follows (taken from Chapter Fifteen of Scharf's book) was at least reviewed by Wood. (The footnotes that originally accompanied Scharf's text have not been included.)*

In the course of his narrative, Scharf twice mentions Lieutenant Francis L. Hoge, another Confederate naval officer who, like John Taylor Wood, found refuge in Halifax for a period after the Civil War.

For other eyewitness accounts by men who served under Wood during his various commando raids, see the annotated bibliography.

THE CAPTURE OF THE USS *UNDERWRITER*

In January, 1864, the Confederate naval commanders at Richmond, Wilmington and Charleston, received orders from the Navy Department to select a boat's crew of fifteen able and trusty seamen, under the command of an experienced officer, from each of the gunboats then lying at the above-named ports, and report with their arms and boats to Commander John Taylor Wood, of the C.S. navy, and Colonel on the President's staff, at Wilmington, N.C. By the latter part of January everything was in readiness; the men were well armed, and accompanied by four boats and two large launches, they left Wilmington by the Kingston railway, under the command of Col. Wood. The utmost secrecy had been observed by those in command as to the object of the expedition and its destination.

The town of Newberne, a place of some note in North Carolina, lies on a point of land at the junction of the Trent and Neuse Rivers with Pamlico Sound. Roanoke Island was captured on the 14th of February, 1862, and following that event Newberne surrendered to the Federals. They at once threw up fortifications, which extended over an area of twenty miles, and in order to strengthen their position and provide against the chances either of surprise or capture, three or four of their gunboats were either anchored off the wharf at Newberne, or else kept cruising up and down the Neuse or Trent Rivers. The largest of these gunboats was the *Underwriter*, a large side-wheel steamer, which fired the first gun in the attack on Roanoke Island, and participated in most of the engagements fought along the North Carolina coast. The *Underwriter* had engines of 800 horse power, and carried four guns, one six-inch rifled Dahlgren, one eight-inch of the same pattern, one twelve-pound rifle, and one twelve-pound howitzer. Jacob Westervelt, of New York, Acting Master U.S. navy, was her commander.

The expedition under Col. Wood reached Kingston early on the morning of Sunday, January 31st; the boats being at once unloaded from the cars and dragged by the men to the river and launched in the Neuse. The distance between Kingston and Newberne by rail is about thirty miles, but the tortuous and circuitous course which the river takes, makes the journey by water at least twice that length. Bending silently to the muffled oars, the expedition moved down the river. Now, the Neuse broadened until the boats seemed to be on a lake; again, the tortuous stream narrowed until the party could almost touch the trees on either side. Not a sign of life was visible, save occasionally when a flock of wild ducks, startled at the approach of the boats, rose from the banks, and then poising themselves for a moment overhead, flew on swift wing to the shelter of the woodland or the morass. No other sound was heard to break the stillness save the constant, steady splash of the oars and the ceaseless surge of the river. Sometimes a fallen log impeded the progress, again a boat would run aground, but as hour after hour passed by, the boats still sped on, the crews cold and weary, but yet cheerful and uncomplaining. Night fell, dark shadows began to creep over the marshes and crowd the river; owls screeched among the branches overhead, through which the expedition occasionally caught glimpses of the sky. There was nothing to guide the boats on their course, but the crew still kept hopefully on, and by eleven o'clock the river seemed to become wider, and Col. Wood discovered that he had reached the open country above Newberne.

When in sight of the town, Col. Wood ran his boats into a small stream, and succeeded in getting them close to the shore. The party landed on what seemed to be a little island covered with tall grass and shrubs. Here the men found temporary shelter, and rations were served.

At midnight the men were called to quarters, and the object of the expedition was explained. Major Gen. G.E. Pickett, who was then commanding the Confederate forces operating against Newberne, was to open fire on the enemy's lines around the town, thus drawing his attention inland, while Col. Wood and his command, under cover of the diversion, were, if possible, to capture one or more of the gunboats and clear the river. Arms were inspected and ammunition distributed, and everything made ready to embark on what each of the party felt was a perilous enterprise. In order to distinguish the Confederates in the dark, each man was furnished with a white badge, to be worn around the left arm, and the password "Sumter" was given.

The firing of Pickett's command was now heard on the right. In company with Hoke's brigade, a part of Corse's and Clingham's and some artillery, Gen. Pickett had made a reconnaissance within a mile and a half of Newberne. He met the enemy in force at Batchelor's Creek, killed and wounded about one hundred in all, captured thirteen officers and 280 men, fourteen negroes, two rifled pieces and caissons, 300 stands of small arms, besides camp and garrison equipage. His loss was thirty-five killed and wounded.

While the engagement at Batchelor's Creek was in progress, Acting Volunteer Lieut. G. W. Graves, of the U.S. steamer *Lockwood*, commanding the Federal vessels at Newberne, communicated with Acting Master Westervelt, commanding the *Underwriter*, and Acting Master Josselyn, commanding the *Hull*, ordering them to be in readiness for a move. Early on the morning of the 1st of February, Lieut. Graves ordered the *Underwriter* to get under way and take up position on the Neuse River, so as to command the plain outside of the Federal line of works, and the *Hull* to take a station above her. At 9 A.M. the *Underwriter* had reached the position assigned her, but the *Hull*, soon after getting under way, got aground, and could not be got off during the day. Soon after this, hearing from Gen. J.W. Palmer, in command of the Union forces, that the Confederates were planting a battery near Brice's Creek, Lieut. Graves, in the *Lockwood*, proceeded as far up the Trent River as he could get, and laid there for the night.

In the meantime, Col. Wood had again launched his boats in the Neuse, and arranged them in two divisions, the first commanded by himself, and the second by Lieut. B.P. Loyall. After forming parallel to each other, the two divisions pulled rapidly down stream. When they had rowed a short distance, Col. Wood called all the boats together, final instructions were given, and this being through with, he offered a fervent prayer for the success of his mission. It was a strange and ghostly sight, the men resting on their oars with heads uncovered, the commander also bareheaded, standing erect in the stern of his boat; the black waters rippling beneath; the dense overhanging clouds pouring down sheets of rain, and in the blackness beyond an unseen bell tolling as if from some phantom cathedral. The party listened — four peals were sounded and then they knew it was the bell of the *Underwriter*, or some other of the gunboats, ringing out for two o'clock. Guided by the sound, the boats pulled toward the steamer, pistols, muskets and cutlasses in readiness. The advance was necessarily slow and cautious. Suddenly, when about three hundred yards from the *Underwriter*, her hull loomed up out of the inky darkness. Through the stillness came the sharp ring of five bells for half-past two o'clock, and just as the echo died away, a quick, nervous voice from the deck hailed, "Boat ahoy!" No answer was given, but Col. Wood kept steadily on. "Boat ahoy! Boat ahoy!!" again shouted the watch. No answer. Then the rattle on board the steamer sprang summoning the men to quarters, and the Confederates could see the dim and shadowy outline of hurrying figures on deck. Nearer Col. Wood came, shouting, "Give way!" "Give way, boys, give way!" repeated Lieut. Loyall and the respective boat commanders, and give way they did with a will. The few minutes that followed were those of terrible suspense. To retreat was impossible, and if the enemy succeeded in opening fire on the boats with his heavy guns all was lost.

The instructions were that one of the Confederate divisions should board forward and the other astern, but, in the excitement, the largest number of the boats went forward, with Col. Wood amidships.

In the meantime, the *Underwriter*, anchored within thirty yards of two forts, slipped her cable and made efforts to get up sufficient steam from her banked fires, to move off, or run the Confederates down. This movement only hastened the boarding party, and the crews pulled rapidly alongside. Lieut. George W. Gift, believing that the *Underwriter* was moving, gave orders to Midshipman J. Thomas Scharf, who was in command of the boarders in the bow of his launch, to open fire on the steamer with the howitzer which was mounted in the bow, and endeavor to cripple her machinery. One shot was fired which struck in the pilot house, and before the howitzer was reloaded the boats were alongside, and the crews scrambling on deck. The enemy had by this time gathered in the ways just aft of the wheel-house, and as the Confederates came up they poured into them into them volley after volley of musketry, each flash of which reddened the waters around, enabling the attacking party to note their position. In spite of the heavy fire, the boarders were cool and yet eager, now and then one or more were struck down, but the rest never faltered. When the boats struck the sides of the *Underwriter*, grapnels were thrown on board, and the Confederates were soon scrambling, with cutlass and pistol in hand, to the deck with a rush and a wild cheer, that rung across the waters, the firing from the enemy never ceasing for one moment. The brave Lieut. B.P. Loyall was the first to reach the deck, with Engineer Emmet F. Gill, and Col. Wood at his side. Following in their steps came Lieuts. Francis L. Hoge, Wm. A Kerr, Philip Porcher, James M. Gardner, F.M. Roby, Henry Wilkinson, George W. Gift, Midshipmen Saunders, H.S. Cook, J.T. Scharf, and William S. Hogue, gallantly leading their men.

The firing at this time became so hot that it did not seem possible that more than half the Confederates would escape with their lives. Col. Wood, with the bullets whistling around him, issued his orders as coolly and unconcernedly as if the enemy had not even been in sight. All fought well. There was no halting, no cowardice; every man stood at his post and did his duty. The conduct of the officers was beyond all praise. Cool and collected in every movement, they executed their parts well. From Commander Wood down to the youngest midshipman, not one faltered. Conspicuous among all was the conduct of the marines, a company of them under Capt. Thomas S. Wilson being distributed through the boats. As the Confederates came up to the ship the marines rose and delivered their fire, taking accurate aim, reloading still under the heavy fire from the enemy. When on board they obeyed their orders promptly, and, forming on the hurricane deck, not even the explosion of the monster shell fired by the enemy from one of the shore batteries among them could break the ranks or turn a man from his post.

Once on the deck of the *Underwriter* the onslaught was furious. Cutlasses and pistols were the weapons of the Confederates, and each selected and made a rush for his man. The odds were against the attacking party, and some of them had to struggle with three opponents. But they never flinched in the life-and-death struggle, nor did the gallant enemy. The boarders forced the fighting. Blazing rifles had no terrors for them. They drove back the enemy inch by inch. Steadily, but surely, the boarders began to gain the deck, and crowded their opponents to the companion-ways or other places of concealment; while all the time fierce hand-to-hand fights were going on on other portions of the vessel. Now, one of the Confederates would sink exhausted — again, one of the enemy would fall on the slippery deck. Rifles were snatched from the hands of the dead and the dying, and used in the hands as bludgeons did deadly work. Down the companion-ways the attacked party were driven pell-mell into the ward-room and steerage, and even to the coal-bunkers, and after another sharp but decisive struggle the enemy surrendered. The *Underwriter* was captured, its commander slain, and many of its officers and men killed and wounded, or drowned. The Confederate loss was over one-fourth of the number engaged — six killed and twenty-two wounded. E.F. Gill, the Confederate engineer, lay in the gangway mortally wounded, and Midshipman Saunders, a gallant boy, cut down in a hand-to-hand fight, breathed out his young life on the deck.

The *Underwriter* was moored head and stern between Fort Anderson and Fort Stevenson, and scarcely a stone's throw from the shore. The sound of the firing was heard at the batteries, and by the time the Confederates captured the boat, which took about ten minutes, the Federals on shore fired a shell into her, which struck the upper machinery and exploded on deck. All of the shore batteries then opened fire on the doomed vessel, either careless of or not realizing the fact that their own wounded must be on board; and the captors soon found that a rapid movement would have to be made. The prisoners were ordered into the boats, and the Confederates who were on board began to prepare for action. Lieut. Hoge opened the magazines and manned the guns. Steam, however, was down and the machinery disabled, and with a heavy fire from the batteries pouring upon them, it was seen that the Confederates could not take sufficient time to carry off their prize. It was, therefore, determined to set fire to the vessel. The Confederate wounded and those of the enemy were carefully removed to the boats alongside, the guns were loaded and pointed towards the town, fire was applied from the boilers, and in five minutes after the boarders left, the *Underwriter* was in one mass of flames from stem to stern, burning with her the dead bodies of those of the brave antagonists who had fallen during the action.

The Confederates retired under a heavy fire from the shore batteries, and also from a volley of musketry, which whistled along the water. They turned once more up the Neuse, and pulled away from the town. As they rounded a point of woods they took a last look at the burning steamer, now completely enveloped in flame, the lurid light flaming in the sky and flashing for miles across the water. Although hidden from view, they could see by sudden flashes in the sky, and by the dull, heavy booming sound which came to them upon the night air, that the shell-room was reached and that the explosion had begun. Turning into Swift Creek, about eight miles from Newberne, the party landed on the shore to care for the wounded and receive intelligence from Gen. Pickett. It was part of the Confederate plan, if the military had been successful in their attack upon the enemy's works on the land side of Newberne, for the boats to land a large force of infantry on the water side of the forts and to attempt to carry them by assault. Owing to the failure of some of his command to co-operate in the demonstration, Gen. Pickett withdrew his troops from before Newberne, and the naval force, on the next morning, retired up the river.

During the attack on the *Underwriter*, which was defended with great gallantry, the other gunboats took the alarm and made up the Trent as fast as steam could carry them, and luckily for the Confederates they did not dare to take part in the fight. When the shell exploded on the deck of the *Underwriter*, it is said that Acting Master Westervelt, the commander, leaped overboard, and was killed hanging to a hawser. Edgar G. Allen, the engineer of the *Underwriter*, who escaped, in his report to Lieut. Graves, under date of February 2d, 1864, says:

"I, together with eighteen or twenty of the crew, being put into the whale boat belonging to the *Underwriter*.... We then shoved off and were proceeding up the stream, the boat I was in being astern the rest, when I discovered that, in their hurry to get off, they had only put two men as guard in the boat. This fact I discovered by the one in the stern steering (by whom I was sitting) hailing the other boats, which were some fifty yards ahead of us, and asked them to take off some of us, as the boat was so overloaded it could make no headway, and also saying they wanted a stronger guard, as all but two were prisoners. One of the other boats was turning to come back, when I snatched the cutlass from the belt of the guard and told the men to pull for their lives. Some of the men, the other guard among them, jumped overboard and swam for the land. I headed the boat for the shore and landed at the foot of the line of breastworks, delivered my prisoner to the commanding officer, and procuring an ambulance, took one of our disabled men to the hospital."

The *Underwriter* lost in the engagement about nine killed, twenty wounded and nineteen prisoners. Twenty-three of her officers and men escaped.

In recognition of the distinguished gallantry displayed in the capture of the *Underwriter*, the Confederate Congress, on February 15th, 1864, unanimously passed the following:

"*Joint resolution of thanks to Commander John Taylor Wood and the officers and men under his command, for their daring and brilliant conduct.*

"*Resolved, by the Congress of the Confederate States of America,* That the thanks of the Congress of the Confederate States are due, and are hereby tendered, to Commander John Taylor Wood, Confederate States Navy, and to the officers and men under his command, for the daring and brilliantly executed plans which resulted in the capture of the U.S. transport schooner *Elmore*, on the Potomac River; of the ship *Alleghany*, and the U.S. gunboats *Satellite* and *Reliance*; and the U.S. transport schooners *Golden Rod*, *Coquette* and *Two Brothers*, on the Chesapeake; and more recently, in the capture from under the guns of the enemy's works of the U.S. gunboat *Underwriter*, on the Neuse River, near Newberne, North Carolina, with the officers and crews of the several vessels brought off as prisoners."

"This was a rather mortifying affair for the navy" (U.S.) says Admiral Porter, "however fearless on the part of the Confederates. This gallant expedition," he continues, "was led by Commander John Taylor Wood.... It was to be expected that with so many clever officers who left the Federal navy and cast their fortunes with the Confederates, such gallant actions would often be attempted," and it is his opinion that "had the enemy attacked the forts the chances are they would have been successful, as the garrison was unprepared for an attack from the river, their most vulnerable side."

Appendix 2

United States Vessels Captured by the CSS *Tallahassee*

Date (1864)	Vessel	Type	Disposition
11 August	*Sarah A. Boyce*	schooner	scuttled
11 August	*James Funk*	pilot boat	burned
11 August	*Carrie Estelle*	brig	burned
11 August	*Bay State*	bark	burned
11 August	*A. Richards*	brig	burned
11 August	*Carroll*	schooner	bonded
11 August	*William Bell*	pilot boat	burned
12 August	*Atlantic*	schooner	burned
12 August	*Adriatic*	schooner	burned
12 August	*Suliote*	bark	bonded
12 August	*Spokane*	schooner	burned
12 August	*Billow*	brig	scuttled
12 August	*Robert E. Packer*	schooner	bonded
13 August	*Glenarvon*	bark	scuttled
13 August	*Lamont DuPont*	schooner	burned
14 August	*James Littlefield*	ship	scuttled
15 August	*Mary A. Howes*	schooner	scuttled
15 August	*Howard*	schooner	scuttled
15 August	*Floral Wreath*	schooner	scuttled
15 August	*Sarah B. Harris*	schooner	bonded
15 August	*Restless*	schooner	scuttled
15 August	*Etta Caroline*	schooner	scuttled
16 August	*P.C. Alexander*	bark	burned

Date (1864)	Vessel	Type	Disposition
16 August	*Leopard*	schooner	burned
16 August	*Pearl*	schooner	burned
16 August	*Sarah Louise*	schooner	burned
16 August	*Magnolia*	schooner	burned
17 August	*North America*	schooner	scuttled
17 August	*Neva*	brig	bonded
17 August	*Josiah Achom*	schooner	burned
17 August	*Diadem*	schooner	released
17 August	*D. Ellis*	schooner	released
20 August	*Roan*	brig	burned

Total: 33 vessels (16 burned, 10 scuttled, 5 bonded, 2 released)

Appendix 3

A Song for the Forecastle

"A Song for the Forecastle" was written by the Southern poet E. King, the self-styled "Naval Song Writer of the South." Written "for the C.S. Fleet," the song appears in a transcript in the microfilmed scrapbook that forms part of the John Taylor Wood papers at the University of North Carolina. The song most likely dates from August 1864 and was probably copied from a Southern newspaper.

King was the author of the best-known piece of sheet music relating to the Confederate Navy: The Alabama; Respectfully Dedicated to the Gallant Captain Semmes, His Officers, and Crew, and to the Officers and Seamen of the C.S. Navy *(Richmond: Geo. Dunn & Compy. [sic], c. 1864), which featured music by F.W. Rosier.*[227] *Apparently "A Song for the Forecastle" was never published in a separate edition.*

For the Crew of the Tallahassee:

A SONG FOR THE FORECASTLE

We are Southern Sailors bold and free
And fear no Invading Northern foe;
With our gallant little fleet
We will chase them o'er the deep
And we'll fight them wherever we go;

Chorus:
For our cause is just
And in God we'll trust
To Give us the victory

Our Country's summons we'll obey,
And her Flag gaily fling to the breeze;
And with a sailor's pride,
We'll brave both wind and tide,
As defiant we sail o'er the seas.

No "Yankee" shall e'er pollute our soil,
Nor a Port shall he find on our strand;
For like Tars both brave and true,
We'll show "Yankee doodle do"
How to die for our dear native Land.

Appendix 4

An Annotated Checklist of the Published and Unpublished Writings of John Taylor Wood

The following chronological listing of Wood's published and unpublished writings does not cover his letters (including his published letters to the editor) or his diaries. Nor does it include the reports and other material by him found in the Official Records of the Union and Confederate Navies in the War of the Rebellion *(1894–1927).*

1. [History of the Confederate States Navy], (c. 1880)
   [An eight-page summary history of the Confederate States Navy prepared for Jefferson Davis and enclosed with a letter to Davis dated 26 December 1880. This document was described in a calendar of Davis' post-war manuscripts that was published by the Louisiana Historical Association in 1943; however, it is now apparently missing from the Davis papers held by Tulane University.]

2. "The First Fight of Iron-Clads," *The Century Illustrated Monthly Magazine* XXIX, 5 (March 1885)
   [Wood's first published memoir devoted to his Civil War experiences. A slightly abridged and revised version of the piece appeared in the first book of the four-volume collection *Battles and Leaders of the Civil War* (New York: Century Co., 1887-1888) edited by Robert U. Johnson and Clarence C. Buel.]

3. "Running the Blockade at Halifax," *Halifax Carnival Echo* (5–10 August 1889)
   [Wood's first published account of the cruise of the *Tallahassee*. This text

was later reprinted under the title "Blockade Running from Halifax" in the *Halifax Herald* (13 November 1899)]

4. [Military Record of J. Taylor Wood], (May 1890)
   [A three-page summary by Wood of his military career. This document was enclosed with a letter to Varina Davis dated 15 May 1890. This unpublished text is found in the Davis papers held by Tulane University.]

5. "Escape of the Confederate Secretary of War," *The Century Illustrated Monthly Magazine* XLVII, 1 (November 1893)
   [Wood's third Civil War memoir, recounting his post-war escape to Cuba. The piece also appeared, with minor revisions, in the anthology *Famous Adventures and Prison Escapes of the Civil War* (New York: Century Co., 1904). Recently the text was reprinted in the *Civil War Times Illustrated* XL, 6–7 (December 2001-February 2002).]

6. [Lee and His Generals], (15 January 1897)
   [The first of two Civil War–related papers that Wood delivered to the Philomathic Society of Dalhousie College. While notices regarding this paper have been located, no copy of the text, which included some autobiographical material, has been found.]

7. "A Cruise on a Blockade Runner," *The Evening Mail* (14 February 1898)
   [The first part of a paper on the *Tallahassee's* cruise that Wood delivered to the Philomathic Society of Dalhousie College on 11 February. This portion of the text was also published in the *Halifax Herald* (15 February 1898). Curiously, the second part of Wood's paper, which was announced for publication in both the *Mail* and the *Herald*, never appeared.]

8. "The Cause of the Disaster," *The Halifax Herald* (22 February 1898)
   [Under this title the *Herald* gathered a number of brief front-page articles on the sinking of the USS *Maine*, including a brief piece by Wood speculating on the probable cause of the explosion.]

9. "The *Tallahassee's* Dash into New York Waters," *The Century Illustrated Monthly Magazine* LVI, 3 (July 1898)
   [Wood's third — and best-known — account of the cruise of the *Tallahassee*. The text was later reprinted in the pamphlet *The "Tallahassee's" Dash into New York Waters* (Suffolk, VA: Robert Hardy Publications, 1987).]

10. "Halifax, the Open Door of Canada," *The Canadian Magazine* XXII, 6 (April 1899)
    [A brief survey of Halifax's history and advantages as a port.]

11. "The Capture of a Slaver," *Atlantic Monthly* LXXXVI, DXVI (October 1900)
    [Wood's reminiscences of his service in the suppression of the slave trade

on board the brig *Porpoise*. The article also appeared in the Halifax *Evening Mail* (20 October 1900).]

12. *Reminiscences of John Taylor Wood*, (c. 1902–1904)
[This unfinished, thirty-five-page autobiographical text, which covers the first twenty years of Wood's life, was found in his office in Halifax following his death in 1904. Sometime later, probably in the 1920s or 1930s, his daughter, Lola Wood, issued a number of mimeographed copies that included some editorial notes by her. The author of the present volume owns one of these mimeographed copies.]

13. "Veteran of Three Navies," *The Halifax Herald*, November 1904
[Wood's account of the career of his friend William Hall, a black Nova Scotian and Victoria Cross-winner who served in the American, British, and Chinese navies. The typescript of this text was acquired after Wood's death by his friend Major B.R. Ward of the Royal Engineers. Following a flurry of correspondence about Hall in the Halifax newspapers, Ward submitted Wood's text to the *Herald* for publication. The piece was probably written in 1902.]

Notes

Chapter 1: A Forgotten Confederate Colony

1. Very little has been written about the post-war exodus of Confederate refugees to Canada, probably because so many of the Southern expatriates eventually returned to America. Far more attention has been paid to the Confederate exile experience in Mexico, South America, and Central America, where more permanent colonies were established. See, for example, Alfred Jackson Hanna and Kathryn Abbey, *Confederate Exiles in Venezuela* (Tuscaloosa: Confederate Publishing, 1960); Andrew F. Rolle, *The Lost Cause: The Confederate Exodus to Mexico* (Norman: University of Oklahoma Press, 1965); William Clark Griggs, *The Elusive Eden: Frank McMullan's Confederate Colony in Brazil* (Austin: University of Texas Press, 1987); David P. Werlich, *Admiral of the Amazon: John Randolph Tucker, His Confederate Colleagues, and Peru* (Charlottesville and London: University Press of Virginia, 1990); Alicja Iwanska, *British American Loyalists in Canada and U.S. Southern Confederates in Brazil: Exiles from the United States* (Lewiston, NY and Queenstown, ON.: Edwin Mellen Press, 1993); and Donald C. Simmons, *Confederate Settlements in British Honduras* (Jefferson, NC: McFarland, 2001).

2. See relevant biographical entries in Richard N. Current, ed., *Encyclopedia of the Confederacy*, vols. 1–4 (New York: Simon and Schuster, 1993).

3. Lt.-Col. George Taylor Denison, *Soldiering in Canada: Recollections and Experiences* (Toronto: Morang, 1900), 58–82.

4. Arthur Thurston, *Tallahassee Skipper* (Yarmouth, N.S.: Lescarbot Press, 1981), 357–364; Greg Marquis, *In Armageddon's Shadow: The Civil War and Canada's Maritime Provinces* (Montreal and Kingston: McGill-Queen's University Press, 1998), 274–278.

5. For the most thorough discussion of Halifax's connection with the Civil War, see Marquis, *In Armageddon's Shadow*. Also see Greg Marquis, "The Ports of Halifax and Saint John and the American Civil War," *The Northern Mariner/Le Marin du nord* VIII, 1 (January/janvier 1998): 1–19; Francis I.W. Jones, "A Hot Southern Town: Confederate Sympathizers in Halifax During the American Civil War," *Journal of the Royal Nova Scotia Historical Society*, vol. 2 (Halifax: Royal Nova Scotia Historical Society, 1999), 52–69.

6. For information on Confederate operations in British North America, see *inter alia* John Headley, *Confederate Operations in Canada and New York* (New York and Washington: Neale Publishing, 1906); Robin W. Winks, *Canada and the United States:*

The Civil War Years (Baltimore: Johns Hopkins Press, 1960); Oscar A. Kenchen, *Confederate Operations in Canada and the North: A Little-Known Phase of the American Civil War* (North Quincy: Christopher Publishing House, 1970); Mason Philip Smith, *Confederates Downeast: Confederate Operations in and Around Maine* (Portland: The Provincial Press, 1985); and Marquis, *In Armageddon's Shadow.*

    7. Thurston, *Tallahassee Skipper*, pp. 357–364; Marquis, *In Armageddon's Shadow*, 203–206, 274–278.

Chapter 2: Early Life, 1830–1847

    8. Private collection of the author, John Taylor Wood, "Reminiscences of John Taylor Wood," 1. This 35-page mimeographed text was copied, probably in the 1920s or 1930s, by Wood's daughter, Lola, from a typescript found among Wood's papers following his death in 1904. Lola Wood made an unknown number of copies, likely for limited distribution among family members. These mimeographed copies included a few notes by Lola Wood, as well as a number of her corrections. In a brief introductory note, Lola Wood indicated that the original typescript had been transcribed — with numerous typographical errors — by her father's office boy from a holograph manuscript. The author's copy of the mimeographed text was acquired in 1997 from an Indiana bookseller and is the only known extant copy. For the purposes of quotation, obvious spelling and punctuation errors have been corrected. The document represents the beginning portion of an unfinished autobiography and covers Wood's life from his early childhood through to the spring of 1851. Royce Shingleton's excellent study of Wood's war career, *John Taylor Wood: Sea Ghost of the Confederacy* (Athens: University of Georgia Press, 1979), only briefly touches on Wood's early life (see pp. 2–4). Shingleton, who did not have access to Wood's autobiographical manuscript, readily admits that his book should not be viewed as a full-fledged biography (p. xii). See also Thurston, *Tallahassee Skipper*, 34–35. Thurston's disjointed, speculative, and meandering book is generally less reliable than Shingleton's biography; nonetheless, it does include some valuable information about Wood, particularly relating to Nova Scotia sources.

    9. Wood, "Reminiscences of John Taylor Wood," 2; Shingleton, *John Taylor Wood*, 2–4.

    10. Wood, "Reminiscences of John Taylor Wood," 3.

    11. *Ibid.*, 4–6.

    12. *Ibid.*, 6–7.

    13. *Ibid.*, 7–8.

    14. *Ibid.*, 8.

Chapter 3: United States Navy, 1847–1861

    15. *Ibid.*, 8–10.

    16. *Ibid.*, 10–13.

    17. *Ibid.*, 13–18.

    18. *Ibid.*, 17–18.

    19. *Ibid.*, 19–23

    20. *Ibid.*, 23–27; John Taylor Wood, "Veteran of Three Navies," *Halifax Herald*, 22 November 1904 (see Appendix 3 for a description of this posthumous publication).

21. Wood, "Reminiscences of John Taylor Wood," 27–29.

22. *Ibid.*, 29–30.

23. *Ibid.*, 30–34.

24. *Ibid.*, 35; John Taylor Wood, "The Capture of a Slaver," *Atlantic Monthly* LXXXVI, DXVI (October 1900): 451

25. Wood, "The Capture of a Slaver," 451–456.

26. *Ibid.*, 456–463.

27. WMR [William Morrison Robinson], Jr., "Wood, John Taylor," *Dictionary of American Biography*, vol. 20 (New York: Charles Scribner's Sons, 1936), 465–466; Thurston, *Tallahassee Skipper*, xvi.

28. University of North Carolina at Chapel Hill (hereafter UNC), Wilson Library, Southern Historical Collection #2381, John Taylor Wood Papers, Correspondence.

29. UNC, John Taylor Wood Papers, Correspondence, Wood to Lola Wood, (#100) 9/11/12 August 1859; *Ibid.*, (#106) 11/13/15/17 September 1859; WMR, Jr., "Wood, John Taylor," 465; Shingleton, *John Taylor Wood*, 5; Thurston, *Tallahassee Skipper*, 41–44.

30. UNC, John Taylor Wood Papers, Diary—vol. 1 (1 January 1860–10 January 1861), January–February, 1860; Shingleton, *John Taylor Wood*, 5–6.

31. UNC, John Taylor Wood Papers, Diary—vol. 1 (1 January 1860–10 January 1861), March–June, 1860; Shingleton, *John Taylor Wood*, 6–9; Thurston, *Tallahassee Skipper*, 48–50.

32. UNC, John Taylor Wood Papers, Diary—vol. 1 (1 January 1860–10 January 1861), August–November, 1860; Thurston, *Tallahassee Skipper*, 51–52.

33. UNC, John Taylor Wood Papers, Diary—vol. 1 (1 January 1860–10 January 1861), December 1860; *Ibid.*, vol. 2 (11 January–4 September 1861), January–March, 1861; Shingleton, *John Taylor Wood*, 9–15; Thurston, *Tallahassee Skipper*, 55–57.

34. UNC, John Taylor Wood Papers, Diary—vol. 2 (11 January–4 September 1861), April 1861; Shingleton, *John Taylor Wood*, 15–17; Thurston, *Tallahassee Skipper*, 57–58.

35. UNC, John Taylor Wood Papers, Diary—vol. 2 (11 January–4 September 1861), April–August, 1861; Shingleton, *John Taylor Wood*, 18–19; Thurston, *Tallahassee Skipper*, 59–60

36. UNC, John Taylor Wood Papers, Diary—vol. 2 (11 January–4 September 1861), August–September, 1861; *Ibid.*, Scrapbook; Shingleton, *John Taylor Wood*, 19; Thurston, *Tallahassee Skipper*, 59.

Chapter 4: Confederate States Navy, 1861–1865

37. Mary Alice Wills, *The Confederate Blockade of Washington, D.C., 1861–1862* (Parsons, WV: McClain Printing, 1975).

38. Tulane University Manuscripts Department (hereafter TUMD), Louisiana Historical Association Collection, Jefferson Davis Papers (55-D), untitled enclosure with a letter from John Taylor Wood to Varina Davis, 15 May 1890.

39. Wills, *The Confederate Blockade of Washington, D.C., 1861-1862*, 127–133.

40. John Taylor Wood, "The First Fight of Iron-Clads," *The Century Illustrated Monthly Magazine*, XXIX, 5 (March 1885): 740–741.

41. John Taylor Wood, "The First Fight of Iron-Clads," 742.

42. *Ibid.*, 744.

43. *Ibid.*, 746.

44. *Ibid.*, 753.

45. *Ibid.*

46. *Ibid.*

47. J. Thomas Scharf, *History of the Confederate States Navy from Its Organization to the Surrender of Its Last Vessel* (New York: Rogers and Sherwood, 1887), 708–718; John M. Coski, *Capital Navy: The Men, Ships and Operations of the James River Squadron* (Campbell, California: Savas Publishing Company, 1996), 41–49.

48. Shingleton, *John Taylor Wood*, 52–61; Thurston, *Tallahassee Skipper*, 148–152.

49. UNC, John Taylor Wood Papers, Correspondence, Wood to Lola Wood, 5 July 1862.

50. United States Department of the Navy, *Official Records of the Union and Confederate Navies in the War of the Rebellion* ser. 2, vol. 2 (Washington: Government Printing Office, 1894–1927) [hereafter cited as *ORN*], 256–257, Wood to Catesby Jones, 30 August 1862.

51. Confederate States of America, *Journal of the Congress of the Confederate States of America, 1861–1865*, vol. 2 (Washington: Government Printing Office, 1904–1905), 386, 402.

52. "Col. John Taylor Wood," *Confederate Veteran* 12, 9 (September 1904): 451–452.

53. *ORN*, ser. 1, vol. 5,118–119; Scharf, *History of the Confederate States Navy*, 122, n. 2; UNC, John Taylor Wood Papers, Correspondence, Wood to Lola Wood, 1–6 October 1863; Shingleton, *John Taylor Wood*, 62–65.

54. *ORN*, ser. 1, vol. 5, 137–141, 346; *Ibid.*, ser. 1, vol. 8, 161–169; Shingleton, *John Taylor Wood*, 65–69.

55. *ORN*, ser. 1, vol. 5, 140, Welles to Commodore Harwood, 17 November 1862.

56. *Journal of the Congress of the Confederate States of America, 1861–1865*, vol. 3, 33, 60.

57. UNC, Wood Papers, Scrapbook, Jefferson Davis to Wood, 9 February 1863.

58. TUMD, Jefferson Davis Papers (55-D), encl. with letter from Wood to Varina Davis, 15 May 1890.

59. *ORN*, ser. 1, vol. 8, 859–860, Wood to Jefferson Davis, 14 February 1863.

60. Shingleton, *John Taylor Wood*, 69–73.

61. *ORN*, ser. 1, vol. 5, 344–345, Wood to Stephen Mallory, 7 September 1863.

62. *Ibid.*

63. Bohemian [William G. Shepardson], "The Capture of Gunboats on the Rappahanock," *Richmond Dispatch*, 2 September 1863; Bohemian [William G. Shepardson], "Close of the Gunboat Raid — Defeat of the Effort to Destroy the Steamers — Brisk Cannonading, &c.," *Richmond Dispatch*, 7 September 1863. For information on Shepardson's journalistic pseudonyms, see J. Cutler Andrews, *The South Reports the Civil War* (Princeton: Princeton University Press, 1970), 448–551.

64. Bohemian, "The Capture of Gunboats on the Rappahanock"; Bohemian, "Close of the Gunboat Raid — Defeat of the Effort to Destroy the Steamers — Brisk Cannonading, &c."; *ORN*, ser. 1, vol. 5, 344–345; Scharf, *History of the Confederate States Navy*, 122–124.

65. *Ibid.*

66. Thurston, *Tallahassee Skipper*, 170.

67. *ORN*, ser. 1, vol. 5, 370–371.

68. *Journal of the Congress of the Confederate States of America, 1861–1865*, vol. 3, 461, 495.

69. TUMD, Jefferson Davis Papers (55-D), encl. with letter from Wood to Varina Davis, 15 May 1890.

70. Scharf, *History of the Confederate States Navy*, 396.

71. Daniel B. Conrad, "Capture and Burning of the Federal Gunboat 'Underwriter,' in the Neuse, off Newbern, N.C., in February, 1864," *Southern Historical Society Papers*, vol. XIX (Richmond: Southern Historical Society,1893), 93–94

72. Scharf, *History of the Confederate States Navy*, 396.

73. Conrad, "Capture and Burning of the Federal Gunboat 'Underwriter,' in the Neuse, off Newbern, N.C., in February, 1864," 94–95.

74. Benjamin P. Loyall, "Capture of the *Underwriter*," *Southern Historical Society Papers*, vol. XXVII (Richmond: Southern Historical Society,1896), 138.

75. Shingleton, *John Taylor Wood*, 103.

76. Scharf, *History of the Confederate States Navy*, 397.

77. *Ibid.*

78. Scharf, *History of the Confederate States Navy*, 400; Loyall, "Capture of the *Underwriter*," 140.

79. Loyall, "Capture of the *Underwriter*," 142.

80. *The War of the Rebellion: A Compilation of the Official Records of the Union and Confederate Armies in the War of the Rebellion* (Washington: Government Printing Office, 1880–1901) [hereafter cited as *OR*], ser. 1, vol. 33, 92–94, General George E. Pickett to Robert E. Lee, 15 February 1864 (with report enclosed); *Ibid.*, 102–103, Wood to Robert E. Lee, February 18, 1864; Shingleton, *John Taylor Wood*, 105–110; William R. Trotter, *Ironclads and Columbiads: The Civil War in North Carolina; The Coast* (Winston-Salem: John F. Blair, 1989), 228–231.

81. Robert E. Lee, *Lee's Dispatches: Unpublished Letters of General Robert E. Lee, C.S.A., to Jefferson Davis and the War Department of the Confederate States of America, 1862–1865, from the Private Collection of Wymberley Jones de Renne, of Wormsloe, Georgia* (New York: G.P. Putnam's Sons, 1915) ed. Douglas Southall Freeman, 136.

82. *Journal of the Congress of the Confederate States of America, 1861–1865*, vol. 3, 747.

83. David D. Porter, *The Naval History of the Civil War* (New York: Sherman,1886), 472.

84. TUMD, Jefferson Davis Papers (55-D), encl. with letter from Wood to Varina Davis, 15 May 1890; Shingleton, *John Taylor Wood*, 112–115; Trotter, *Ironclads and Columbiads*, 233–252.

85. *OR*, ser. 1, vol. LI, pt. 2, 870, Wood to Davis, 21 April 1864.

86. Shingleton, *John Taylor Wood*, 116.

87. Wood, "Veteran of Three Navies."

88. TUMD, Jefferson Davis Papers (55-D), encl. with letter from Wood to Varina Davis, 15 May 1890; *ORN*, ser. I, vol. 10, 721.

89. Shingleton, *John Taylor Wood*, 116–117.

90. TUMD, Jefferson Davis Papers (55-D), encl. with letter from Wood to Varina Davis, 15 May 1890.

91. *Ibid*; *ORN*, ser. I, vol. 10, 721–722.

92. John Taylor Wood, "The Tallahassee's Dash into New York Waters," *The Century Illustrated Monthly Magazine* LVI, 3 (July 1898): 409; Naval History Division, Navy Department, *Civil War Naval Chronology* (Washington: GPO, 1971), VI-309–311.

93. UNC, John Taylor Wood Papers, Scrapbook, Stephen Mallory to Wood, 23 July 1864.

94. Wood, "The Tallahassee's Dash into New York Waters," 409–410.

95. *Ibid.*, 410.

96. *Ibid.*, 411.

97. Bohemian [William G. Shepardson], "The Cruise of the 'Tallahassee' [1]," *Richmond Dispatch*, 19 September 1864.

98. Wood, "The Tallahassee's Dash into New York Waters," 412.

99. *Ibid.*, 413.

100. Bohemian [William G. Shepardson], "The Cruise of the 'Tallahassee' [2]," *Richmond Dispatch*, 23 September 1864. The only known photograph of the *Tallahassee*, taken in Halifax harbor by the photographer Isaac Parish, clearly shows the vessel's broken mainmast. Parish, who was active in Halifax from 1862 to 1869, printed and sold copies of this photograph as a carte-de-visite. For a discussion of Parish's career in Halifax, see Jim Burant, "Pre-Confederation Photography in Halifax, Nova Scotia," *The Journal of Canadian Art History* IV, 1 (Spring 1977): 41.

101. *ORN*, ser. 1, vol. 3, 705–706, Wood to Mallory, 6 September 1864.

102. For a full account of the diplomatic intrigue that swirled around the *Tallahassee* during her visit to Halifax, see Marquis, *In Armageddon's Shadow*, 222–240. Also see *Correspondence Relating to the "Tallahassee"* ([Halifax: King's Printer,1865]). It has been suggested that the CSS *Tallahassee* was actually involved in a secret Southern plan to invade New England. This improbable scenario likely derives from Confederate disinformation. See James Horan, *Confederate Agent: A Discovery in History* (New York: Crown Publishers, 1954), 115, 228; Philip Van Doren Stern, *Secret Missions of the Civil War* (Chicago: Rand, McNally, 1959), 219–220; William A. Tidwell, *April '65: Confederate Covert Action in the American Civil War* (Kent, OH and London, England: Kent State University Press, 1995), 136.

103. Shortly before his death, Wood authenticated a chart tracing his precise route out of Halifax harbor. See Nova Scotia Archives and Records Management (hereafter NSARM), Maps, HO 2320 (negative # 8974). Also see note 197 below.

104. Wood, "The Tallahassee's Dash into New York Waters," 416.

105. Marquis, *In Armageddon's Shadow*, 233–234.

106. John Taylor Wood, "Running the Blockade at Halifax," *Halifax Carnival Echo*, 5–10 August 1889.

107. Wood, "The Tallahassee's Dash into New York Waters," 416–417.

108. Bohemian, "The Cruise of the 'Tallahassee' [2]."

109. For information on Battery Wood, see Coski, *Capital Navy*, 169–170. For King's song, see Appendix 3. Also see Thurston, *Tallahassee Skipper*, 208.

110. Mary Boykin Chesnut, *Mary Chesnut's Civil War* (New Haven and London: Yale University Press, 1981), ed. C. Vann Woodward, 639.

111. Wood, "The Tallahassee's Dash into New York Waters," 416–417.

112. Jefferson Davis, *The Rise and Fall of the Confederate Government*, vol. 2 (New York: Appleton, 1881), 265.

113. ORN, ser. 1, vol. 10, 747, Lee to Seddon, 22 September 1864.

114. *Ibid.*, 783, Vance to Davis, 14 October 1864.

115. *Ibid.*, pp. 793–794, Mallory to Davis, with attached memo from Davis to Wood, 22 October 1864.

116. *Ibid.*, 801–802, Davis to Vance, 25 October 1864.

117. John Wilkinson, *The Narrative of a Blockade-Runner* (New York: Sheldon & Co., 1877), 211.

118. Wood, "Veteran of Three Navies." For more on Hewett's Civil War career, see Stephen R. Wise, *Lifeline of the Confederacy: Blockade Running During the Civil War* (Columbia: University of South Carolina Press, 1988), 109, 196–198, 354. In 1862, when the Confederate commissioners James Mason and John Sliddell were released from Fort Warren, it was Hewett, as commander of HMS *Rinaldo*, who transported them from Massachusetts. Hewett first attempted to take the Southern dignitaries to Halifax, but extremely foul weather forced him to reverse his course and steam to Bermuda. See James D. Richardson, *A Compilation of the Messages and Papers of the Confederacy,*

Including the Diplomatic Correspondence, 1861–1865 (Nashville: United States Publishing Company 1905), vol. II, 162–165, J.M. Mason to Hon. R.M.T. Hunter, 2 February 1862.

119. Wood, "Veteran of Three Navies."

120. Coski, *Capital Navy*, 159–162, 196–197.

121. ORN, ser. 1, vol. 11, 803, Mallory to Mitchell, 21 January 1865.

122. For a full account of the Battle of Trent Reach, see Coski, *Capital Navy*, 194–210.

123. TUMD, Jefferson Davis Papers (55-D), encl. with letter from Wood to Varina Davis, 15 May 1890.

124. *Journal of the Congress of the Confederate States of America, 1861–1865*, vol. 4, 537, 545.

125. UNC, John Taylor Wood Papers, Diary — vol. 3 (2 April–16 July 1865), 10.

Chapter 5: Escape to Cuba, 1865

126. For further information on Wood's role in the selection and preservation of Davis' papers, see Douglas Southall Freeman, *The South to Posterity: An Introduction to the Writing of Confederate History* (New York: Charles Scribner's Sons, 1939), 96–101.

127. UNC, John Taylor Wood Papers, Diary — vol. 3 (2 April–16 July 1865), 1–3.

128. Captain Robert E. Lee, *Recollections and Letters of General Robert E. Lee* (Westminister: Archibald, Constable & Company, 1904), 357.

129. UNC, John Taylor Wood Papers, Diary — vol. 3 (2 April–16 July 1865), 4.

130. *Ibid.*, 5–6; Shingleton, *John Taylor Wood*, 150–154.

131. UNC, John Taylor Wood Papers, Diary — vol. 3 (2 April–16 July 1865), 6–10; Shingleton, *John Taylor Wood*, 154–155.

132. UNC, John Taylor Wood Papers, Diary — vol. 3 (2 April–16 July 1865), 10–14; Shingleton, *John Taylor Wood*, 156.

133. UNC, John Taylor Wood Papers, Diary — vol. 3 (2 April–16 July 1865), 15–16; A.J. Hanna, *Flight into Oblivion* (Richmond: Johnson Publishing Company, 1938), 85–93.

134. UNC, John Taylor Wood Papers, Diary — vol. 3 (2 April–16 July 1865), 16–24; Hanna, *Flight into Oblivion*, 99–101; Shingleton, *John Taylor Wood*, 159–162.

135. Hon. John H. Reagan, "Flight and Capture of Jefferson Davis," in *The Annals of the War Written by Leading Participants North and South* (Philadelphia: Times Publishing Co., 1879), 156.

136. Davis, *Rise and Fall of the Confederate Government*, vol. 2, 702.

137. Wood, "Escape of the Confederate Secretary of War," *The Century Illustrated Monthly Magazine* XLVII, 1 (November 1893), 110. For more on the "underground passage" utilized by fleeing Confederates, see Hanna, *Flight into Oblivion*, 125–150.

138. Wood, "Escape of the Confederate Secretary of War," 110–111.

139. *Ibid.*, 111.

140. *Ibid.*

141. *Ibid.*, 111–112.

142. *Ibid.*, 112.

143. *Ibid.*, 112–113.

144. *Ibid.*, 113; UNC, John Taylor Wood Papers, Diary — vol. 3 (2 April–16 July 1865), 47–50.

145. Wood, "Escape of the Confederate Secretary of War," 113–114; UNC, John Taylor Wood Papers, Diary — vol. 3 (2 April–16 July 1865), 50–52.

146. Wood, "Escape of the Confederate Secretary of War," 115; Wood, "Reminiscences of John Taylor Wood," 5–8.
147. Wood, "Escape of the Confederate Secretary of War," 115–116.
148. *Ibid.*, 116.
149. *Ibid.*, 116–118.
150. *Ibid.*, 118–119.
151. *Ibid.*, 119–121.
152. *Ibid.*, 121; Hanna, *Flight into Oblivion*, 182–184.
153. Wood, "Escape of the Confederate Secretary of War," 121–122.
154. *Ibid.*, 122–123; Hanna, *Flight into Oblivion*, 187.
155. Wood, "Escape of the Confederate Secretary of War," 123; Hanna, *Flight into Oblivion*, 187–188.
156. Wood, "Escape of the Confederate Secretary of War," 123; Hanna, *Flight into Oblivion*, 188–190.

Chapter 6: Exile in Halifax, Nova Scotia, 1865–1904

157. UNC, John Taylor Wood Papers, Diary — vol. 3 (2 April–16 July 1865), 66–69.
158. *Ibid*, 69–71.
159. *Ibid*, 68.
160. Thurston, *Tallahassee Skipper*, pp. 357–364; Marquis, *In Armageddon's Shadow*, 274–278.
161. Hereward Senior, *The Last Invasion of Canada: The Fenian Raids, 1866–1870* (Toronto and Oxford: Dundurn Press, 1991), 45–57; Harold A. Davis, "The Fenian Raid on New Brunswick," *The Canadian Historical Review* XXXVI, 4 (December 1955): 316–334.
162. The text of the petition from the Halifax-area Confederates is found in Thurston, *Tallahassee Skipper*, 358–359. Unfortunately, Thurston does not provide a citation for the document, and research at NSARM in Halifax and at the National Archives of Canada (hereafter NAC) in Ottawa has failed to reveal the original source. However, the covering letter, from Benjamin Wier to Premier Charles Tupper, which accompanied the petition, is found in the Tupper papers at the NAC. See Sir Charles Tupper fonds, MG 26 F, vol. 2, 721–723, Wier to Tupper, 19 March 1866. Wier's letter indicates that the petition was delivered to him by Wood.
163. NSARM, MG 1, vol. 14, Almon Scrapbook, 86.
164. *Ibid.*, 98; David A. Sutherland, "Wood, John Taylor," *Dictionary of Canadian Biography*, vol. XII (Toronto: University of Toronto Press, 1994), 1110–1111; Allan E. Marble, "Almon, Johnston William," *Dictionary of Canadian Biography*, vol. XII (Toronto: University of Toronto Press, 1994), 16–17.
165. Sutherland, "Wood, John Taylor," 1111; *The Nova Scotian*, 22 July 1904; *McAlpine's Nova Scotia Directory for 1868-69* (Halifax: David McAlpine, 1868), 444; Shingleton, *John Taylor Wood*, 206.
166. Sutherland, "Wood, John Taylor," 1111; *The Nova Scotian*, 22 July 1904.
167. UNC, John Taylor Wood Papers, Scrapbook.
168. Sutherland, "Wood, John Taylor," 1111. Even after the failure of Wood and Company, the firm's wharf continued to be known as Wood's Wharf for many decades.
169. UNC, John Taylor Wood Papers, Scrapbook; *The Nova Scotian*, 22 July 1904.; Sutherland, "Wood, John Taylor," 1111; Shingleton, *John Taylor Wood*, 204–205.
170. Letter from W.B. Sturtevant, "The Log Book," *Sea Stories Magazine* X, 4

(June 1925): 185–186. For a full account of the *Herbert Fuller* mutiny, see Thomas H. Raddall, *Footsteps on Old Floors: True Tales of Mystery* (Garden City: Doubleday, 1968), 43–94.

171. Erhard, *First in Its Class: The Story of the Royal Nova Scotia Yacht Squadron* (Halifax: Nimbus Publishing, 1986), 41–44, 144, 151.

172. For more on Wood's Halifax residence, see Marian Moore, "Group Tours 'Victorian' Home," Halifax *Mail-Star*, 17 March 1964; Barbara Hinds, "Demolishing Link With Brave Seadog," Halifax *Mail-Star*, 15 March 1969. Wood's home was torn down in 1969 to make room for a parking lot.

173. *The Nova Scotian*, 22 July 1904.

174. *Ibid*; Henry James Morgan, *The Canadian Men and Women of the Time: A Hand-book of Canadian Biography of Living Characters; Second Edition* (Toronto: William Briggs, 1912), 1183; NAC, RG 18, vol. 3438, service file 0.54, Z.T. Wood.

175. Halifax *Herald*, 13 and 18 November 1899; Annie Elizabeth Mellish, *Our Boys Under Fire: Canadians in South Africa* (Charlottetown, PEI: s.n., 1900), 15–16.

176. UNC, John Taylor Wood Papers, Family Notes, transcripts of letters from Arthur Davison to Wood, 8–9 December 1899; *Ibid*., Correspondence, Robert E. Lee [Jr.] to Wood, 25 November 1899.

177. Thurston, *Tallahassee Skipper*, 379.

178. Charles Bruce Fergusson, *Place-Names and Places of Nova Scotia* (Halifax: Public Archives of Nova Scotia, 1967), 121.

179. Wood, "Veteran of Three Navies;" David W. States, "William Hall, V.C., of Horton Bluff, Nova Scotia, Nineteenth-Century Naval Hero," *Collections of the Royal Nova Scotia Historical Society*, vol. 44 (Halifax: Royal Nova Scotia Historical Society, 1996), 73, 80–81.

180. UNC, John Taylor Wood Papers, Scrapbook; Thurston, *Tallahassee Skipper*, 369–374; Shingleton, *John Taylor Wood*, 205.

181. *Richmond Dispatch*, 30 May 1890.

182. UNC, John Taylor Wood Papers, Scrapbook; Thurston, *Tallahassee Skipper*, 373–374; Shingleton, *John Taylor Wood*, 205.

183. NSARM, Miscellaneous Manuscripts Collection, vol. 227, item no. 26-d.

184. For a brief survey of this literature, see Gary W. Gallagher, "Introduction," *The Annals of the Civil War Written by Leading Participants North and South* (New York; Da Capo Press, 1994), v–xiv.

185. UNC, John Taylor Wood Papers, Correspondence, William Preston Johnston to Wood, 4 December 1873; TUMD, Jefferson Davis Papers (55-D), enclosure with John Taylor Wood to Davis, 26 December 1880. See Appendix 3 for a full listing of Wood's published and unpublished writings.

186. Shingleton, *John Taylor Wood*, 227–228.

187. See the lists of society members in *Collections of the Nova Scotia Historical Society*, vols. II–VIII (Halifax: Nova Scotia Historical Society, 1881–1895)

188. J. MacDonald Oxley, *Baffling the Blockade* (London, Edinburgh, New York: T. Nelson and Sons, 1896).

189. Alix John [Alice Jones], *The Night-hawk: A Romance of the '60s* (New York: Frederick A. Stokes Company, 1901). The author owns John Taylor Wood's personal copy of this book, inscribed to Wood by Jones.

190. *The Dalhousie Gazette* XXIX, 5 (January 1897): 148.

191. *The Dalhousie Gazette* XXX, 7 (March 1898): 212.

192. See Appendix 4.

193. See Appendix 4.

194. See Appendix 4 and note 8 above.

195. *The Nova Scotian*, 22 July 1904.

196. The original chart authenticated by Wood was once held by the Nova Scotia Museum in Halifax; however, museum staff are no longer able to locate the document. The museum's original acquisition of the chart is documented in *Report on the Provincial Museum, Science Library and Public Records of Nova Scotia, January to September 1929* (Halifax, N.S.: Minister of Public Works and Mines/King's Printer, 1930), 31. Fortunately, a photographic copy of the chart is available at the NSARM (see Maps, HO 2320, negative # 8974). The Maritime Museum of the Atlantic in Halifax, which forms part of Nova Scotia's provincial museum system, does hold an octant and case (accession number M85.77.1) that once belonged to Wood. The octant was originally donated to the Dalhousie University Library's Museum and Treasure Room in the late 1920s by Captain Richard Holland, the Chebucto Head lighthouse keeper, and was later transferred to the provincial museum. Holland's donation is noted in *President's Report for the Year July 1st 1928–June 30th 1929* (Halifax: Dalhousie University, 1929). The Maritime Museum of the Atlantic also owns a naval cutlass (accession number M49.6) that was reportedly presented to someone in Halifax in 1864 by a crew member of the CSS *Tallahassee*.

197. *The Nova Scotian*, 22 July 1904.

198. See note 8 above.

199. "Richard F. Armstrong," *Confederate Veteran* 12, 6 (June 1904): 356. Armstrong is buried, with another Halifax Confederate, Col. Bennett Hornsby, in St. John's Anglican Cemetery in Fairview (Section E, Row 1, Lots 19/20).

200. *The Morning Chronicle*, 22 July 1904.

201. *The Evening Mail*, 19 July 1904.

202. *Acadian Recorder*, 21 July 1904.

203. The Wood family plot comprises Camp Hill Cemetery lots 51 and 52 (off Robie Street in Division UU).

Chapter 7: A Rebel's Legacy

204. See *Nova Scotia Readers; Sixth Book* (London, Edinburgh, Dublin, and New York: Thomas Nelson and Sons, 1906), 180–184. The same excerpt was later reprinted in various editions of *The Atlantic Readers; Sixth Book*, intended for schools in all three Maritime provinces (Nova Scotia, New Brunswick, and Prince Edward Island).

205. Arthur Hunt Chute, "Bluenose Skippers," *Blackwood's Magazine* CCXI, MCCLXXVIII (April 1922): 439–445. Likely inspired, at least in part, by his childhood encounters with Wood, Chute also wrote an intriguing ghost story about a former Confederate privateer commander who turns to piracy after the war. See "The Passing of Mogul Mackenzie," *Blackwood's Magazine* CXCV, MCLXXIX (January 1914): 100–106.

206. Andrew Merkel, *Tallahassee: A Ballad of Nova Scotia in the Sixties* (Halifax: Imperial Publishing Company, 1945).

207. The original Tallahassee School opened in September 1955. A successor school, Tallahassee Community School, was opened in 1992. In September 1994, it became the Tallahassee Primary School. Five years later, it reverted to Tallahassee Community School. Located at 168 Redoubt Way in Eastern Passage, Nova Scotia, it now houses grades primary to three.

208. Anne Travor, *Colorful Confederate Commander and Haligonian John Taylor Wood* (Halifax: Nova Scotia Department of Tourism, c. 1987).

209. See, for example, David Walker, "Did the Tallahassee Escape Through Eastern Passage?," Halifax *Chronicle-Herald*, 1 September 1981; David Harris, "Mystery Shrouds Tallahassee's Departure from Halifax in 1864," *The Mail-Star*, 17 August 1989.

210. For the thesis on Wood, see W.D. Harville, *The Civil War Service of John Taylor Wood* (Dallas: Southern Methodist University, 1935).

211. Davis, *The Rise and Fall of the Confederate Government*, vol. 2, 265.

212. Raimondo Luraghi, *A History of the Confederate Navy* (Annapolis: Naval Institute Press, 1996) [translated by Paolo E. Coletta], 348.

213. John Taylor Wood, "Halifax, the Open Door of Canada," *The Canadian Magazine* XXII, 6 (April 1899): 522.

214. Ulysses S. Grant, *Personal Memoirs of U.S. Grant*, vol. 2 (New York: Charles L. Webster, 1885), 489.

Chapter 8: The First Fight of Iron-Clads

215. The vessel's name is now usually spelled *Merrimack*.

216. The shell from Wood's Brooke rifle struck the observation slit of the *Monitor's* pilothouse, temporarily blinding the commander of the vessel, Lieutenant John L. Worden.

Chapter 9: The Tallahassee's Dash into New York Waters

217. See Chapter 7 and notes 204 and 207 above.

218. Modern sources give the vessel's name as *Atalanta*.

219. Xantippe, the wife of Socrates, was known for her bad temper.

220. Boanerges ("sons of thunder") was the name given by Jesus to James and John, the sons of Zebedee.

221. Businessman and politician Benjamin Wier (1805–1868) served as the Confederate agent in Halifax during the Civil War. See David A. Sutherland's entry on Wier in the *Dictionary of Canadian Biography*, vol. IX (Toronto: University of Toronto Press,1976).

222. William Johnston Almon (1816–1901) was the most prominent Nova Scotian physician identified with the Confederate cause. See Allan Marble's biographical essay on Almon in the *Dictionary of Canadian Biography*, vol. XII (Toronto: University of Toronto Press,1994).

223. See Chapter XX of Sir Walter Scott's *The Legend of Montrose* (1819), in which the garrulous soldier of fortune Dugald Dalgetty becomes so desperate to replenish his wardrobe that he threatens to make clothing from the skin of a fallen comrade.

224. In the *Official Records of the Union and Confederate Navies in the War of the Rebellion* (Washington: Government Printing Office, 1894–1927) the *Tallahassee* is credited with thirty-three captures. See Appendix 2.

Chapter 10: Escape of the Confederate Secretary of War

225. The bulls of the Biblical land of Bashan were noted for their size and strength. See Psalm 22:12.

Appendix 1: The Capture of the USS *Underwriter*

226. Scharf utilizes an earlier variant spelling of this place name, i.e. Newberne. He also refers to Kinston, North Carolina by its original name: Kingston.

Appendix 3: A Song for the Forecastle

227. See T. Michael Parrish and Robert M. Willingham, Jr., *Confederate Imprints: A Bibliography of Southern Publications from Secession to Surrender* (Austin: Jenkins Publishing/Katonah, NY: Gary A. Foster, [1984]), #6793, p. 574.

Annotated Bibliography

Archival Sources

Dalhousie University Libraries System, University Archives. [The University Archives holds a run of *The Dalhousie Gazette*, which includes reports on Wood's two addresses to the Philomathic Society, 1897–1898. The Archives also has a copy of the *President's Report for the Year July 1st 1928–June 30th 1929*, which documents the donation of Wood's Octant to the Dalhousie University Library.]

National Archives of Canada. [The Sir Charles Tupper fonds (in current Canadian archival parlance, an individual's papers are referred to as a "fonds") includes correspondence (MG 26 F, vol. 2) relating to the Fenian petition signed by Wood and other Halifax-area Confederates in 1866. NAC also holds a small Zachary Taylor Wood fonds (MG 30 E 98) as well as his RCMP service file (RG 18, vol. 3438, service file 0.54, Z.T. Wood).]

Nova Scotia Archives and Records Management, Archival Holdings Management Division. [The Almon Scrapbook (MG 1, vol. 14) includes some valuable material relating to Wood and other Halifax-area Confederates. The Miscellaneous Manuscripts Collection includes a file on the CSS *Tallahassee* (vol. 227, no. 26). NSARM also holds a photographic copy of a chart, which Wood authenticated, depicting the *Tallahassee's* precise route out of Halifax harbor (Maps, HO 2320, negative # 8974). Furthermore, the archives has the most comprehensive collection of Halifax newspapers.]

Private collection of the author. [John Taylor Wood, "Reminiscences of John Taylor Wood," a 35-page mimeographed text copied, probably in the 1920s or 1930s, by Wood's daughter Lola from a typescript found among Wood's papers following his death in 1904. The document represents the beginning portion of an unfinished autobiography.]

Tulane University Manuscripts Department, Louisiana Historical Association Collection. [The Jefferson Davis papers include several important letters (some with enclosures) from Wood to Jefferson and Varina Davis.]

University of North Carolina at Chapel Hill, Wilson Library, Southern Historical Collection. [The University of North Carolina holds the most extensive collection of John Taylor Wood papers (# 2381). The manuscripts, which were donated by Wood's daughter Lola, in 1941, consist of four main series: Correspondence (six folders), Diaries (three volumes), Scrapbook, and Family Notes. The latter two series are on microfilm only. Given the fact that Lola Wood retained some archival material, it is possible, if not probable, that a body of Wood-related manuscripts has remained with members of the Wood family.]

Published Sources

Albert, Susan Wingler. "Raider of the High Seas: The Story of John Taylor Wood and the CSS *Tallahassee*," *The United Daughters of the Confederacy Magazine* LIX, 1 (January 1996): 23–26. [A derivative account of the cruise of the CSS *Tallahassee*.]

Anonymous. "Col. John Taylor Wood," *Confederate Veteran* 12, 2 (September 1904): 451–452. [A substantial obituary notice detailing Wood's life and career.]

Anonymous. "Tallahassee Remembered by Admiral," *Trident* 14, 16 (4 September 1980): 1. [A brief retelling of the *Tallahassee's* escape from Halifax.]

"Bohemian" [William G. Shepardson]. "The Capture of Gunboats on the Rappahannock," Richmond *Daily Dispatch* (2 September 1863). [A pseudonymous account of Wood's second Chesapeake raid by William G. Shepardson, a CSN medical officer and journalist who participated in the expedition.]

"Bohemian" [William G. Shepardson]. "Close of the Gunboat Raid — Defeat of the Effort to Destroy the Steamers," Richmond *Daily Dispatch* (7 September 1863). [More on Wood's capture of the USS *Satellite* and the USS *Reliance*.]

"Bohemian" [William G. Shepardson]. "The Cruise of the 'Tallahassee,'" Richmond *Daily Dispatch* (19, 23 September 1864). [A first-hand account of the CSS *Tallahassee's* cruise.]

"Bohemian" [William G. Shepardson]. "The Expedition in North Carolina — The Fight at Newbern," Richmond *Daily Dispatch* (12 February 1864). [An eyewitness description of the seizure of the USS *Underwriter*.]

Borrett, William C. *East Coast Port and Other Tales Told under the Old Town Clock.* Halifax: Imperial Publishing, 1946. [Includes a chapter devoted to the *Tallahassee's* escape from Halifax.]

Butler, Lindley S. *Pirates, Privateers and Rebel Raiders of the Carolina Coast.* Chapel Hill: University of North Carolina Press, 2000. [Wood is one of eight sea raiders examined in this study.]

Campbell, R. Thomas. *Academy on the James: The Confederate Naval School.* Shippensburg, PA: Burd Street Press, 1998. [Contains a chapter on the capture of the USS *Underwriter*.]

Campbell, R. Thomas. *Gray Thunder: Exploits of the Confederate Navy.* Shippensburg, PA: Burd Street Press, 1996. [Includes a chapter on the capture of the USS *Underwriter*.]

Cochrane, Rev. William, ed. *The Canadian Album*, vol. III. Brantford: Bradley,

Garretson & Co., 1894. [Includes a biographical entry on, and photograph of, Wood.]

Congdon, Don, ed. *Combat: The Civil War.* New York: Delacorte Press, 1967. [Includes a substantial excerpt from Wood's "The First Clash of Iron-Clads."]

Conrad, Daniel B. "Capture and Burning of the Federal Gunboat *Underwriter*," *Southern Historical Society Papers,* vol. XXIX. Richmond: Southern Historical Society, 1891. [A first-hand account of the capture of the USS *Underwriter* by the expedition's surgeon.]

Crews, Ed. "Flashing Beacon on the Horizon: One Crisis after Another for a Party of Escaping Confederates," *Military History* 5, 3 (December 1988): 14, 16–17, 56. [Summarizes Wood's account of his escape to Cuba in 1865.]

Dalzell, George W. *The Flight from the Flag: The Continuing Effect of the Civil War upon the American Carrying Trade.* Chapel Hill: University of North Carolina Press, 1940. [This early study of the long-term impact of the Confederate cruisers, includes a chapter on the CSS *Tallahassee.*]

Erhard, Nancie. *First in Its Class: The Story of the Royal Nova Scotia Yacht Squadron.* Halifax: Nimbus Publishing, 1986. [A history of the Royal Nova Scotia Yacht Squadron, which includes a profile of Wood as well as information on his activities as a yachtsman in Halifax.]

Foard, Charles H. "The Confederate States Steamer *Tallahassee*," *Nautical Research Journal* XXI (Summer 1969):72–81. [This article on the warship *Tallahassee* includes copies of the vessel's plans.]

Haliburton, E.D. "The Tallahassee Legend: A Different Tale of Her Exit," Halifax *Chronicle-Herald* (5 October 1981). [A defense of Wood's account of the *Tallahassee's* escape from Halifax in 1864. Written in response to David Walker's revisionist attack on Wood's veracity (see below).]

Hanna, A.J. *Flight into Oblivion.* Richmond: Johnson Publishing Co., 1938. [This study of the post-war fate of the Confederate cabinet contains a good deal of information on Wood's escape to Cuba.]

Harris, David. "Mystery Shrouds Tallahassee's Departure from Halifax in 1864," *The Mail-Star* (17 August 1989). [A brief newspaper article outlining the revisionist challenge to Wood's account of the *Tallahassee's* departure from Halifax.]

Hearn, Chester G. *Gray Raiders of the Sea: How Eight Confederate Warships Destroyed the Union's High Seas Commerce.* Camden, ME: International Marine Publishing, 1992. [This full-scale study of the impact of Confederate raiders on the Union's merchant shipping includes a chapter on the *Tallahassee* and the *Chickamauga.*]

Horan, James D. *Confederate Agent: A Discovery in History.* New York: Crown, 1954. [Contains information on the *Tallahassee's* alleged role in a secret Confederate plan to launch a diversionary attack on Maine.]

Jones, Charles Lucian. "The Naval Expedition from Wilmington, North Carolina, and the Cruise of the C.S. Steamer *Tallahassee*," *Addresses Delivered Before the Confederate Veteran's Association of Savannah, Georgia, 1898–1902* (Savannah: The Association, 1902). [An account of the *Tallahassee's* cruise by the vessel's paymaster.]

Jones, Francis I.W. "A Hot Southern Town: Confederate Sympathizers in Halifax

During the American Civil War," *Journal of the Royal Nova Scotia Historical Society*, vol. 2. Halifax: Royal Nova Scotia Historical Society, 1999. [Provides information on the main source for the revisionist challenge to Wood's account of the *Tallahassee's* departure from Halifax through the Eastern Passage.]

Jones, Hervey W. "The 'Tallahassee' Eludes Pursuers," *The Open Gateway* I, 3 (April 1931): 16–17, 20–21. [An article on the cruise of the *Tallahassee* and Wood's subsequent career in Halifax.]

Louisiana Historical Association. *Calendar of the Jefferson Davis Postwar Manuscripts*. New York: Burt Franklin, 1970. [Provides useful summaries of Wood's correspondence with Jefferson Davis.]

Lownds, Russell. *The Sea, Ships and Sailors: Stories of the Sea in and Around Nova Scotia*. Halifax, N.S: Petheric Press, 1970. [Includes a chapter on Wood and the *Tallahassee*.]

Loyall, Benjamin P. "Capture of the *Underwriter*," *Southern Historical Society Papers*, vol. XXVII. Richmond: Southern Historical Society, 1899. [A memoir of the capture of the *Underwriter*.]

Luraghi, Raimondo. *A History of the Confederate Navy*. Annapolis: Naval Institute Press, 1996. (Translated by Paolo E. Coletta). [This authoritative history of the Confederate States Navy includes a chapter on naval commandos, much of which is devoted to Wood.]

Marquis, Greg. *In Armageddon's Shadow: The Civil War and Canada's Maritime Provinces*. Montreal & Kingston: McGill-Queen's University Press, 1998. [This definitive study of the impact of the Civil War on the Maritime provinces of British North America offers a thorough account of the diplomatic intrigue that surrounded the cruise of the CSS *Tallahassee*. The book also provides much information on Confederate sympathizers in Nova Scotia and Confederate operations and activities in the Maritime region.]

Merkel, Andrew. *Tallahassee: A Ballad of Nova Scotia in the Sixties*. Halifax: Imperial Publishing Company, 1945. [A long narrative poem that not only tells the story of the CSS *Tallahassee*, but also examines the impact of the American Civil War on Nova Scotia.]

Moebs, Thomas Truxton. *Confederate States Navy Research Guide*. Williamsburg: Moebs Publishing Company, 1991. [Contains some useful information relating to Wood. Purports to reprint J. Thomas Scharf's sketch of Wood's career from *History of the Confederate Navy from Its Organization to the Surrender of its Last Vessel*, but actually neglects to include most of the text.]

[Nova Scotia. Lieutenant Governor.] *Correspondence Relating to the "Tallahassee."* [Halifax: King's Printer, 1865.] [A compilation of the official correspondence pertaining to the visit of the CSS *Tallahassee* to Halifax.]

O'Driscoll, Patricia E. "Ship with Seven Names," *Sea Breezes* 19, 110 (February 1955): 134–135. [The story of the vessel that, for a time, was known as the CSS *Tallahassee*.]

Piers, Harry, comp. *Biographical Review; Province of Nova Scotia*. Boston: Biographical Review Publishing Co., 1900. [Includes an entry on Wood.]

Raddall, Thomas H. *The Significance of "Tallahassee."* Halifax: Imperial Publishing Company, 1945. [Small promotional brochure reprinting Raddall's review of Andrew Merkel's *Tallahassee: A Ballad of Nova Scotia in the Sixties*.]

Robbins, Peggy. "By Land and by Sea," *Civil War Times Illustrated* XXXVII, 1 (March 1998): 42–45, 53–56, 59. [An account of Wood's military career, with emphasis on his activities as the Confederacy's "horse marine."]

Robinson, William M., Jr. "Wood, John Taylor," *Dictionary of American Biography*, vol. 20. New York: Charles Scribner's Sons, 1936. [A brief early account of Wood's career.]

Rutherford, Phillip. "The New Bern Raid," *Civil War Times Illustrated* XX, 9 (January 1982): 8–15. [An account of Wood's raid on New Bern and the capture of the USS *Underwriter*. Reproduces the same misattributed photograph of John Taylor Wood that appeared in two of Royce Gordon Shingleton's articles on Wood (see below).]

Scharf, J. Thomas. *History of the Confederate Navy from Its Organization to the Surrender of Its Last Vessel*. New York: Rogers and Sherwood, 1887. [Includes a biographical sketch of Wood as well as accounts of several of his missions as a raider.]

Shingleton, Royce Gordon. "Confederate Commando: John Taylor Wood's Raid on New Berne," *Civil War* VIII, 6 (November–December 1990): 12–17, 74–75. [A detailed account of Wood's New Berne raid. Includes a photo that is mistakenly identified as a portrait of Wood.]

Shingleton, Royce Gordon. "Cruise of the CSS *Tallahassee*," *Civil War Times Illustrated* XV, 2 (May 1976): 30–40. [An article describing the *Tallahassee's* nineteen-day cruise up the Atlantic coast in August 1864. Includes the same misattributed portrait of Wood that is noted above.]

Shingleton, Royce Gordon. *John Taylor Wood: Sea Ghost of the Confederacy* (Athens: The University of Georgia Press, 1979). [The most detailed and accurate account of Wood's military career.]

Shingleton, Royce Gordon. "Raider's Blow Stinging," *Military History* 6, 5 (December 1990): 38–44. [An account of Wood's activities as a raider in Chesapeake Bay in 1863. Reprinted in *Great Battles* VIII, 4 (May 1995): 26–32.]

Shingleton, Royce Gordon. "Swashbuckler in Gray: The Confederate Service of John Taylor Wood," *The United Daughters of the Confederacy Magazine* XLI, 10 (October 1978): 18–19. [A short survey of Wood's career.]

Shingleton, Royce Gordon. "Wood, John Taylor," *Encyclopedia of the Confederacy*, vol. 4. New York: Simon and Schuster, 1993. [A brief sketch of Wood's career.]

Shingleton, Royce Gordon. "Wood, John Taylor," *American National Biography*, vol. 23. New York: Oxford University Press, 1999. [A short biography of Wood.]

Smith, Mason Philip. *Confederates Downeast: Confederate Operations in and Around Maine*. Portland: The Provincial Press, 1985. [Includes a chapter on the Confederate raiders *Tallahassee* and *Florida*.]

Stern, Philip Van Doren. *Secret Missions of the Civil War*. Chicago: Rand McNally, 1959. [Includes an abridged version of Wood's account of the voyage of the *Tallahassee*.]

Sutherland, David A. "Wood, John Taylor," *Dictionary of Canadian Biography*, vol. XII. Toronto: University of Toronto Press, 1994. [A useful biographical essay on Wood.]

Taylor, John M. "From Virginia to Tallahassee: Career of a Confederate Raider," *America's Civil War* 10, 1 (March 1997): 46–52. [A short account of Wood's eventful military career. Subsequently reprinted in William N. Still, Jr., John M. Taylor, and Norman C. Delaney, *Raiders and Blockaders: The American Civil War Afloat* (Dulles, VA: Brassey's, 2000)].

Thomas, Mary Elizabeth. "The C.S.S. *Tallahassee*: A Factor in Anglo-American Relations, 1864–1865," *Civil War History* 21 (June 1975): 148–159. [An examination of the impact of the *Tallahassee's* cruise on diplomatic relations between England and the United States.]

Thurston, Arthur. *Tallahassee Skipper*. Yarmouth: Lescarbot Press, 1981. [A meandering and ultimately unreliable biography of Wood, which, despite its many shortcomings, does contain some useful information. In 1988-1999, Thurston issued a so-called revised edition of his book. It consists of copies of the original printing with some additional, photocopied notes pasted to the inside front covers and the title pages.]

Travor, Anne. *Colorful Confederate Commander and Haligonian John Taylor Wood*. Halifax: Nova Scotia Department of Tourism, c. 1986. [A brief account of Wood's life prepared for a tourism campaign aimed at American Civil War enthusiasts. In addition to appearing as a separate brochure, this text was also published in one or more U.S. Civil War magazines as part of an advertising section placed by the province of Nova Scotia.]

Trotter, William R. *Ironclads and Columbiads: The Civil War in North Carolina; The Coast*. Winston-Salem, NC: John F. Blair, Publisher, 1989. [Includes a chapter detailing Wood's involvement in the Confederate combined operation against Union forces at New Bern, North Carolina.]

United States Department of the Navy. *Official Records of the Union and Confederate Navies in the War of the Rebellion* (31 vols. divided into two series). Washington: Government Printing Office, 1894–1927. [An invaluable source on Wood's wartime career. Documents written by him, or which refer to him, are found in series I, vols. 2–3, 5, 7–12, 15 and series II, vols. 1–3.]

Wakelyn, Jon L. *Biographical Dictionary of the Confederacy*. Westport, CT: Greenwood Press, 1977. [Includes an entry on Wood's career.]

Walker, David A. "Did the Tallahassee Escape Through Eastern Passage?," Halifax *Chronicle-Herald* (1 September 1981). [A rather lame challenge to the veracity of Wood's account of the *Tallahassee's* departure from Halifax in 1864.]

Wood, John Taylor — *See Appendix 4 for a full listing of Wood's writings.*

Index

173